Praise for *Do Penguins Eat Peaches?*

If you're poised to launch your own business, this is the book for you. Nothing is more important than understanding your customer, and *nothing* is what you'll achieve if you don't. *Do Penguins Eat Peaches?* gives example after example of why market research is vital to business success and how you can put it into practice.

Nick North CMRS, Director of Audiences, BBC

There has never been a more vital time to know and connect with customers. When small business owners have intense competition for their attention, market research can get left behind. In this book Katie Tucker advises *that* is not wise! The book comes complete with encouragement and top tips on how to get closer to customers and secure the all-important sales. It's a must-read for any modern-day small business owner.

Emma Jones CBE, founder of Enterprise Nation

A super-relevant read for businesses of all sizes. Katie Tucker simplifies and demystifies the world of customer research and provides real practical steps on how to use it to make better business decisions. *Do Penguins Eat Peaches?* reminds us that understanding what customers really want should be at the heart of everything businesses do.

Nick Unsworth, Vice President of Strategic Partnerships and Business Development, Getty Images

I highly recommend this book for anyone looking for a valuable resource on how to understand your customers. *Do Penguins Eat Peaches?* is straightforward, easy to understand and practical. Katie provides great examples that help illustrate the concepts and make them more relatable. This book is a must-read for anyone looking to improve market research knowledge and skills, and it is perfect for both beginners and experts alike.

Jeremy Weil, Head of Product at the Economist Intelligence Unit (EIU), *The Economist*

As a founder, one skill will help you succeed almost more than any other. And that is to ask the questions that no one else is asking. So you arrive at the answer that no one else could. Understanding customers is all about asking the right questions. That is how you will win. This book will teach you that precious skill.

David Hieatt, co-founder of The Do Lectures and Hiut Denim Co, and author of *Do Purpose* and *Do Open*

This book is a must-gift for entrepreneurs everywhere. Katie offers a secret sauce for business growth: uncovering what customers really want.

Diana Kander, *New York Times* bestselling author of *All in Startup* and keynote speaker on Curiosity

Packed with insights, *Do Penguins Eat Peaches?* is the ultimate guide for solopreneurs, start-ups and small businesses who want to up their market research game. Levelling the playing field between the big dogs and the underdogs, this book will supercharge your customer discovery, sharpen your decision making and drive success. Forget the need for a big team or budget – Katie's got your back!

Tom Sutton, founding partner of SEED VC and Seed Ready, co-founder and CTO of Chase Interaction

Katie has so much to teach small businesses – I use the lessons she's taught me every single day when I'm engaging with my customers and online audience. If you want to stop guessing and making mistakes and start creating products and services people really want to buy – read this book.

Helen Perry, host of the Just Bloody Post It Podcast and marketing teacher for creatives

This book is a must-read for all small businesses. Packed with practical advice on how to understand customers so you can build products and services that sell.

Tim Adler, Group Editor of Small Business, Growth Business and Information Age at Stubben Edge

This book is an essential resource for anyone who wants to succeed in today's business environment either on or offline. This book provides a comprehensive guide to conducting market research, including how to identify your target market, collect and analyse data, and use the insights gained to improve your strategies and sales. Full of actionable tips and strategies for finding customers. From leveraging social media to building a referral network, *Do Penguins Eat Peaches?* provides a wealth of ideas and insights on how to reach and engage with your target audience.

Phil Teasdale, CEO of Enterprise Made Simple and author of *The Blue Whale Plan*

This is the book all business owners need to read. Insightful, witty and packed full of thought-provoking moments that really get you thinking about your customers and how to connect with them. This isn't just a book about customer research but a bible of anecdotal insights for people who want to understand their audience and know how to connect with them on a level that drives real and tangible results.

Lara Sheldrake, community expert, speaker, consultant and founder of Found & Flourish

Clear, punchy and actionable, Katie's book will make you feel empowered to do the work of market research AND make sense of whatever you find out. For a copywriter, the big win is learning to speak your customer's language. The easy-to-action tasks in this book will help you supercharge your marketing.

Dr Susan Moore, copywriter, messaging strategist and founder of Virtual Gold Dust

Being a feedback-focused micro-business owner is less daunting with this book by your side. Katie has a knack for demystifying jargon and making customer research seem doable and *gasp* exciting. This book is going to have so many dog-eared pages, Post-it notes sticking out the top, and margin notes, I just know it.

Jo McCarthy, online shop mentor and founder of Firain

Katie makes market research accessible and easy to understand. This book is written in an engaging and uplifting way with lots of actionable tips. A good read for any business owner!

Anniki Sommerville, marketing consultant and author of
The Big Quit: How to ditch the job you hate and find work you love

Do Penguins Eat Peaches? is a much-needed book. It levels the playing field between larger corporations, who often have better access to resources and know-how, and smaller businesses and entrepreneurs. Filled with practical advice and examples, this book will radically change the way you see your customers.

Jane Frost CBE, and CEO of the Market Research Society (MRS)

Lively and thought-provoking writing that provides insight, inspiration and practical tips for anyone in the community and public sectors who needs to better understand their customers.

Paul Ely, independent greenspace and leisure consultant

Katie Tucker

do

penguins

eat

peaches?

**and other unexpected
ways to discover what
your customers want**

First published in Great Britain by Practical Inspiration Publishing, 2023

© Katie Tucker, 2023

The moral rights of the author have been asserted

ISBN   9781788604178 (print)
       9781788604192 (epub)
       9781788604185 (mobi)

Every effort has been made to trace copyright holders and to obtain their permission for the use of copyright material. The publisher apologizes for any errors or omissions and would be grateful if notified of any corrections that should be incorporated in future reprints or editions of this book.

Want to bulk-buy copies of this book for your team and colleagues? We can customize the content and co-brand *Do Penguins Eat Peaches?* to suit your business's needs.

Please email info@practicalinspiration.com for more details.

Practical Inspiration
Publishing

Dedication

To Aidan and Grace. Be curious. Question everything.

Table of contents

List of stretch tasks

Stretch task #1: How well do you know your customers?
This stretch task helps you answer this question by identifying what you know, what you think you know and what you need to find out.

Stretch task #2: Are you speaking your customers' language?
Make sure your messages are landing with your target audience by asking them a few simple questions.

Stretch task #3: Practise being wrong
A few suggestions to use in everyday life to strengthen your 'being wrong' muscle. It doesn't have to be painful.

Stretch task #4: Find eight customers to speak to in record time
Tap into your people network to find out who you can talk to.

Stretch task #5: Make time for market research
A short planning exercise to ensure the research gets done.

Stretch task #6: Identify your values to help navigate business decisions
Figure out your values to help you make good choices.

Preface

This book started with a rejection. I entered Practical Inspiration Publishing's (PIP) business book challenge in May 2020 during the first UK COVID-19 lockdown. Ten days to write a book proposal alongside a bunch of fellow aspiring authors.

I'd recently returned from a family gap year. I'd quit my corporate job. I'd named my yet-to-be-a-real-business business: Product Jungle®. That was it.

Under PIP founder Alison Jones' expert eye, we squirmed, wrote and re-wrote. We worked hard and asked ourselves even harder questions. At the end, we emerged with a business book proposal ready to send out into the world. It was a competition. One lucky proposal won a traditional publishing deal with PIP. It wasn't mine.

You only realize how much you want something when you don't get it. So, I persevered. I took on all the feedback and slowly started work on my business and my book. Amid career changes and the toll of lockdown parenting, I kept going. Every six months, I would send Alison an update. Sometimes I'd get a response, sometimes not (publishers are busy people).

By this time, I was adamant that I needed to write this book. Small businesses all around me were passionate but struggling to bring in consistent sales. They worried and were often confused about which ideas to pursue next. I knew I could help.

Two years later, I got the email I'd been waiting for: the deal for the book you're reading right now. I needed to find a title, one that would pique your curiosity (did it?). If you love a backstory, here's what happened:

> I couldn't start this book without the title. I'm the kind of person who needs a roof before building what's inside. Some sort of container, a lid, to let the rest flow.

> I finally found the title one evening, as I lay sprawled on the floor waiting for my daughter to fall asleep. With a pen in one hand and a scrap of paper in the other, I wrote down every idea I could muster in the moment.

> Do Penguins Eat Peaches? was the last idea on my list. There was something audacious about it. Curious. Pushing us to think beyond the obvious. Do they eat peaches? Our assumption? Probably not. But has anyone ever asked?

> *And, well… alliterations make me happy.*

> What's in a title? Intrigue. Surprise. Curiosity. In a crowded space, we judge a book by its cover.

> I tested it and a majority loved it. Some liked it and others were puzzled, preferring the other two front-runners.

> 'Not sure about that one, it's kind of different,' one person said. 'I think I prefer the second one.' Long pause. Hesitation. 'What was the second one again?'

> Whether they loved it, liked it or would've chosen something else. Everyone remembered it.

And just like that I'd found my roof. Dear reader, I hope you'll remember it too.

Extract from Jungle Juice*, 13th June 2022

Katie Tucker
London 2023

*Jungle Juice is my popular weekly email read by hundreds of businesses, helping them understand customers better. Come find out all about it on page xxiii. Sign up at www.productjungle.co.uk/newsletter or use the QR code on the following page.

Jungle Juice

- The first Jungle Juice newsletter was sent on 6th September 2021 to 48 businesses.
- Today, it's read by hundreds of businesses ranging from independent creatives and makers, freelancers, product and services businesses, start-ups and consultants to product managers and C-suite executives.
- *Freshly squeezed ideas, stories and inspiration to help you understand your customers better* is the Jungle Juice strapline and I deliver on that promise every week.
- Over 60% of subscribers regularly open Jungle Juice (proud as peach punch with that stat!).
- Readers' favourites include Are you an Askhole?[1], Don't bring toddlers to Buddhist temples[2] and The answer to most of your problems.[3]
- Jungle Juice covers a vast array of topics including how to ask customers better questions, how to fit in market

---

[1] Are you an Askhole? https://www.productjungle.co.uk/campaigns/view-campaign/are-you-an-askhole

[2] Don't bring toddlers to Buddhist temples. https://www.productjungle.co.uk/campaigns/view-campaign/dont-bring-toddlers-to-buddhist-temples

[3] The answer to most of your problems. https://www.productjungle.co.uk/campaigns/view-campaign/the-answer-to-most-of-your-problems

research, how to test a business idea and how to make better business decisions.

- Jungle Juice gets regular feedback such as 'You're hilarious Katie. Great message to read on a Monday morning like all your emails!', 'I love your newsletter. Thanks for the great tips and content. You're an inspiration', 'As always, fantastic!' and 'Excellent as usual Katie.'
- What are you waiting for? Come join us! We're having a blast.

Come join us. Sign up at www.productjungle.co.uk/newsletter

Foreword

Market research is fascinating. It's fascinating because it's all about people. The way they interact with each other, with products, with ideas, with everything. People are fascinating because they are complex and frequently changing. The worst thing a business or entrepreneur can do is to make assumptions on what people want based on personal behaviour, what their mates in the pub or fellow parents at the school gates say, or what they saw on Twitter.

I have spent my career building brands and creating change based on deep and sometimes radical understanding of customer behaviour. I know the power of evidence and actionable insight to get the backing of the budget holder, the operations director, the CFO or bank manager. Now, as CEO of the world's oldest professional association for market research, MRS, I am privileged to see the best and the worst of research come across my desk. Research doesn't have to be expensive, but it does have to be right. The right methodology, the correct analysis and the right narrative to deliver a real understanding of the choices that businesses can make.

Many products or businesses aren't differentiated by function (what they do) but by the way they do it, by their service ethos, their ethical sourcing, or even their communications. Believe me when I say that communication in these days of message overload is vital. So, when Katie, as a member of MRS, came to me to tell me about her book, *Do Penguins Eat Peaches?*, I was sold not just on her arguments and narrative, but on the fact that she had cut through the thousands of different messages we are faced with when it comes to running a business.

The market research sector in the UK is worth over £8 billion and growing. It is fed by a vast number of different needs from government policy and advertising evaluation to product testing. The UK is the starting point for much international research. Part of this success is because of the iterative effect of so many different research needs, part down to the importance of English as a business language, and part down to the fact that the UK has been successfully self-regulated as a profession for almost 70 years. People like Katie and research providers and buyers commit to a code of conduct that ensures professional standards, ethical behaviour and appropriate training.

You don't have to have a huge budget to ensure you have the evidence to make the best decisions for your business – the UK may be large but there are a huge number of free resources available, from the census to case studies and guidance on the MRS website. The UK is also home to a huge number of highly skilled independent professionals who are members of MRS. These are people who can manage an entire project or help you create a survey questionnaire that won't give you false data or perpetuate assumptions.

Do Penguins Eat Peaches? is a much-needed book. It levels the playing field between larger corporations, who often have better access to resources and know-how, and smaller businesses and entrepreneurs. Filled with practical advice, examples, including some I shared with Katie, and guidance on when and where to seek out professional help, this book will radically change the way you see your customers.

**Jane Frost CBE, CEO of the
Market Research Society (MRS), April 2023**

Introduction

I f you're expecting a book about unusual penguin feeding habits, you've picked the wrong book. This is *not* a book about penguins or peaches for that matter. This *is* a book about customer discovery, customer exploration and customer curiosity. It's an invitation to question what you think you know about your audience, your customers, your clients and your community. This book unpicks the assumptions you hold about the people you serve. It shows you how to be brave and how to fail fast. It teaches you how to ask better questions so you can make smarter decisions. *Do Penguins Eat Peaches?* helps you run businesses that stay in business. Businesses people want to buy from.

In other words, this *is* a book about market research. Market research has a serious image problem. Boring. Time consuming. Dated. Collette Doyle, acting editor at the MRS's quarterly magazine *Impact*, hit the nail on the head in an editorial when she wrote: 'Whenever the term pops up... people... tend to picture a grizzled, white-haired gentleman with horn-rimmed glasses, brandishing a clipboard.'[1]

But don't be fooled. Bigger brands are ALL over it. From leading supermarket chains to the ever-imposing tech giants, they are systematically and forensically trying to figure out every move with fancy teams and even fancier tools. And it's easy to see

---

[1] C. Doyle, 'Spread the word' in *Impact*, 38, p. 3 (July 2022).

why. Every dollar invested in understanding customers brings a whopping $100 in return.[2] Bigger companies may be calling it something different. Something with a little more street cred. Customer insight. Customer discovery. Audience analysis. Customer research. User research (UX). Design research. Service design. Customer experience (CX). This book won't be splitting semantic hairs. The fact is understanding customers is an integral part of how successful businesses operate.

Businesses like yours need to do more. Can do more. Just *enough* more. So you too can make smarter decisions, build more robust offerings, stay competitive and reduce the guessing. This book teaches you how.

Who is this book for?

Do Penguins Eat Peaches? is for those of you without big teams and without big budgets, whether you're selling from behind a screen or behind a counter. I wrote this book for you, the lone business owner, the micro-business, the small charity, the self-employed, the freelancer, the SME, and the nascent start-up (always trying to go too fast). But equally, if you stumble upon this book and you work in a big business, stick around. Sometimes *big* should know better but somewhere along the road of back-to-back meetings, aggressive targets and demanding shareholders, *big* can lose its way. Let this book guide you back to your customers.

---

[2] L. Burnam, *32 user experience research statistics to win over stakeholders*, User Interviews (February 2023). Available from: www.userinterviews.com/blog/15-user-experience-research-statistics-to-win-over-stakeholders-in-2020

Democratizing skills for smaller businesses

Given how fundamental customer understanding is to running profitable businesses, I'm stunned at how few books (you'd want to read) are written about market research for us smaller folk. How few, useful, practical resources exist for the thousands of us out there making, creating, teaching, fixing, mentoring, freelancing and consulting. In the UK alone, there are 5.5 million small businesses.[3] Four million of those are solo businesses (no employees). Most business advice centres around levelling up your marketing, branding, selling, copywriting, PR and design (all-important skills). Throw in advice from coaches, courses and mentors on the topics of self-belief, passion and grit, and there you (should) have it: business success. Memorable marketing, savvy social media, top notch branding and palpable passion. You could have all these things, and still your business could flop. Understanding customers is the skill that makes everything else you need to do easier.

The skills and resources on how to understand customers exist and can be applied to your world. But until now, the methods and *savoir faire* have been locked away in corporate boardrooms, academic arenas and jargon-heavy business books. I wrote *Do Penguins Eat Peaches?* to change that. To level the playing field between big and small. I've spent years building a community of small business owners. I've probed and questioned. Surveyed and listened. I understand your challenges. From a lack of sales, lacklustre marketing to the big scary questions of *Will this work?* and *What the hell am I supposed to do next?* I see your overwhelm, your indecision, and this book will help. *Do Penguins Eat Peaches?* distils the essence of successful market research for businesses like you.

---

[3] D. Smith, *How many UK businesses fail in the first year? Startup statistics 2022*, Resolve Financial (2022). Available from: https://www.resolvefinancial.co.uk/startup-failure-statistics

Only the best bits. Promise. By the end of this book, you'll have a solid blueprint for conducting your own market research with practical guidance on what methods to use and how frequently to use them.

This book builds on the foundations of many truly brilliant minds in the business, customer research and behavioural science fields. A myriad of excellent titles exists on understanding customers, building customer-driven strategies, unpicking consumer psychology and improving UX to name a few topics. And I'll be sure to reference the ones relevant to our task in hand: from the candid design consultant, Erika Hall, the applied behavioural economist, Melina Palmer, to customer discovery expert, Teresa Torres. I'll also share the wise words of Steve Blank, Stephen Wunker, Ash Maurya, Travis Lowdermilk and Jessica Rich, as well as draw on some of the frameworks developed by the team behind the innovation consultancy Strategyzer. And then some.

In these pages, you'll also find interviews I was lucky enough to do with Jane Frost CBE, Sara Fortier, Diana Kander, Tamara Milacic, Trina Moore Pervall, Dr Lennart Nacke, Nana Parry, Dana Publicover, Tori Rosevink, Jonny Schneider and Caroline Wilson. All brilliant in their field. They generously shared their wisdom and stories with me. Real people, running real businesses and organizations, and practising what they preach when it comes to understanding customers.

This book is not an exhaustive list of every market research method out there. It will not scientifically argue the statistical pros and cons of sample sizes (plenty of drier books on that topic). Nor will it guarantee the success of your product and service. But this book will give you a fighting chance to delight customers amid the economic uncertainties, the surprise pandemics, the global tensions and the increasingly competitive landscape. Reading and applying what you read in this book will change your mindset, arm you with the right skills and improve your chances of business success.

What is market research and why do we need it?

So, what do we mean by market research? Market research is defined as 'the activity of collecting and studying information about what people want, need and buy.'[4] Pretty foundational stuff when it comes to running a business. The magic comes when you do something with it. Market research helps you plan, prioritize and move beyond your biases. It helps de-risk your ideas and ensures you put things out into the world that delight customers and make money. It's a practice and a skill. Something you can do just enough of to feel more confident.

These days, almost everyone can set up a business. Barriers are low. Technology pretty much free. Business courses and support aplenty. Setting up a business still carries kudos and being your own boss is still glorified. Romanticized, even. Yet so many businesses fold. Sixty percent of small businesses shut shop within their first three years.[5] It's not just bad luck. Or choice (absolutely nothing wrong with throwing in the towel). Businesses fail when they don't sell enough of what they have to offer and when they spot change too late and fail to adapt. At its core, a failing business is one where the numbers no longer add up. Sooner or later, you'll hit a wall. In business post-mortems, journalists write about founders not finding product/market fit. About businesses not solving a problem, finding a pain point, or tapping into a true need or desire. Essentially, when you're flogging a dead horse, all bets are off. In fact, *no market need* (as in nobody wants what you're selling!) is the second most common reason new businesses fail, according to

---

[4] Collins COBUILD Advanced Learner's Dictionary, HarperCollins Publishers. Available from: https://www.collinsdictionary.com/dictionary/english/market-research

[5] D. Smith, *How many UK businesses fail in the first year? Startup statistics 2022*, Resolve Financial (2022). Available from: www.resolvefinancial.co.uk/startup-failure-statistics

business data analytics platform CB Insights.[6] Finding a snug fit between your offer and the market requires more than luck.

Good enough research

So, how do us smaller businesses, with smaller teams and smaller budgets, figure out what our customers want? How do we build and create things people want to consume, buy, and then buy again? How do we innovate? Become more customer-centric? Care more deeply about our customers? And how do we do it, while accepting our small business limitations: time, money and energy. In other words, how do we do good enough research? You don't need to be a behavioural scientist or a professional researcher to understand your customers better. For smaller businesses, good enough is often more than enough. Enough to establish whether you're on the right path or barking up the wrong tree. Enough to keep your ego and biases in check, increase your chances of building and creating things people want, and enough to outsmart your competitors.

There's an argument for investing in research professionals and the services they offer. But a good enough understanding about how to do better surveys, ask better questions, make better customer-driven decisions will strengthen your business foundations and stand you in good stead if and when you decide to call in the pros. You'll know what you're looking for and be better equipped to ask useful questions and select the right partner for you. Win, win.

---

[6] CB Insights, *The top 12 reasons startups fail*, CB Insights (August 2021). Available from: www.cbinsights.com/research/report/startup-failure-reasons-top

In his article 'Finding the Fastest Path to Feedback',[7] consultant, author and speaker Jonny Schneider says:

> Most people are capable of research that is good enough... Remember it only needs to be good enough to inform a decision about what to do next... It's a quest for learning, not a quest for certainty so the consequences of being wrong are pretty low.

I wholeheartedly agree.

How well do you know your customers?

How well do you know your customers now? You're probably doing a yearly survey. Asking for feedback and reviews. Using social media to poll your followers. Checking usage data on your digital channels perhaps. You might be building customer knowledge organically, as you go along. Maybe you're doing even more than this.

But very few of you are asking the right questions. Questions that will help you make better decisions, create better content (we're all content creators these days) and build better products and services. Few of you are leveraging the latest technological advances to eavesdrop on public conversations. Nor are you taking advantage of all the free research available online. Perhaps you don't know how and where to start.

From my experience working with smaller businesses, I believe your relationship to market research is likely to be one of three:

---

[7] J. Schneider, *Finding the fastest path to feedback*, jonnyschneider. com (January 2017). Available from: http://jonnyschneider.com/ fastest-path-to-feedback

- You're doing it intuitively, in anything but name (you're probably a naturally good listener and an empath). Brilliant, but difficult to replicate and scale. Read on, this book will help carve out a repeatable process from your natural qualities.
- You're doing some, but not really getting anything useful and struggling to see the value. This book will give you the right tools and methods to ensure you're getting valuable insights.
- You're not doing it at all. For you, this book will change everything.

Make small your superpower

Being a large business sure has its benefits: more people to do the work, more expertise and more money to spend. But remember small can be incredibly powerful too when it comes to understanding customers. *Small* means you're closer to the people you serve. *Small* means faster decision making. The COVID-19 pandemic highlighted the kindness and nimbleness of small businesses, who were quicker and more considerate to react to changing customer needs. During those trying times, we were rallied to buy small. And we still are. Small business champions such as Mary Portas (aka queen of the high street) and Holly Tucker, founder of notonthehighstreet, are tirelessly speaking up for small, independent businesses and keeping them in the spotlight. Let's ride that wave of support while building strong foundations for our businesses.

On the opposite end of the spectrum, big businesses are under scrutiny for all the wrong reasons. Tax avoidance. Unfair workplace practices. Greedy shareholders. Green washing. Data abuse. They're as popular as a wet summer weekend. Your business isn't like that. It's time to use *small* to your advantage.

How to read this book

This book is a recognition of our times. Busy, fast and distracted. Nobody wants another business book that feels too much like homework. While you can do the stretch tasks dotted throughout this book, you can also *just* read it. My wish is that by the end, the important stuff sticks. That the unexpected things you discover along the way, stay lodged in your brain long after you finish. When you're ready for action, this book, its tasks and templates will still be here, waiting.

In essence, *Do Penguins Eat Peaches?* is an invitation to take a step back and notice what really matters in business: customers. This book will give you a chance to question what you think to be true. You'll finish this book more curious and ready to build new habits that will help your customers and your business.

Some of you will be grazers, preferring to dip in and out of books. You can do that with this book too if you wish. Impatient to get to the practical bits fast? I see you. But do circle back on the first three chapters. That's where we'll bust some myths, unpick assumptions and sharpen our research toolkit. It's where we'll shift your mindset and start building those strong business foundations.

What you'll learn

This book has 13 chapters. Chapter 1 **(I made the front page of *The Sunday Times* and failed, and seven ways market research will improve your business)** kicks off with a wake-up call. Whether you're a small business owner or an employee in a smaller size business, you are not your customer. I'll share a big failure of mine. The time I mistook my own wants and needs with those of my audience, without doing any research. It didn't end well. We'll also look at seven ways market research will improve your business. From launching something new to getting you out of a business funk.

Then things get a little uncomfortable. In Chapter 2 (**Ego, excuses and the fear of failure: what's holding you back?**), we'll tackle why we're *not* doing the work. From market research excuses and myths, the lack of know-how to our pesky ego, and that oh-so-familiar fear of failure.

In Chapter 3 (**The explorer's toolkit: curiosity, empathy and courage**), I'll share three (mental) tools you need to embark on your customer discovery journey: curiosity, empathy and courage. We'll look at how to foster them and how to embody them as you begin your own customer quest.

In Chapter 4 (**I met Alcatraz prisoner 1259, talking to customers and how to just ask**), we'll start getting hands-on. I'll share by far one of the most powerful methods to understand your audience: customer interviews. I'll explain why they're so fruitful and show you how to find people to talk to, how to ask them for their time (introverts I see you) and how to set them up.

Quality questions will be the focus of Chapter 5 (**The mother of all theories and there is such a thing as a stupid question**). My favourite topic. There *is* such a thing as a stupid question when talking to customers. In this chapter, I'll share what questions to avoid and the magic ones that'll bring you actionable insight. I'll also distil a super-useful concept when it comes to understanding customers called Jobs to Be Done (JTBD for short).

In Chapter 6 (**The art and science of sensemaking**), we'll delve into the important task of making sense of all the stuff you'll learn from your customer conversations. All those notes, recordings and transcripts – we'll look at two ways to analyse your insights.

Chapter 7 (**Stop sending shitty surveys**) will cover the nitty gritty of good and bad surveys. It's a quest of mine to stop smaller businesses sending out lazy surveys. It's a waste of time. For you and your customers. There *is* another way.

Feel free to be as lazy as you want, though, in Chapter 8 (**Learn about your customers in your pyjamas and how to win at desk research**) and Chapter 9 (**Can I pick my friend's nose? And how to be a digital spy**), where we'll explore all the wonderful ways you can learn useful stuff about your customers without talking to a soul. From desk research in your pyjamas to the rising power of Artificial Intelligence (AI) and social-listening tools – most of which are absolutely free.

Chapter 10 (**Stop asking for five-star feedback**) will stop you systematically asking for only glowing feedback. How do you move forward in your business if you only want the good stuff? In Chapter 11 (**Small business testing**), I'll give you some quick and dirty ways to test things with customers. Because sometimes the *doing* is the research.

While smaller businesses need to listen to customers, *Do Penguins Eat Peaches?* doesn't advocate being at the mercy of them either. You also have your own goals and values, principles and bandwidth. So, in our penultimate chapter, Chapter 12 (**When not to listen to customers**) we'll explore specifically when not to pay attention to a word they say.

In our last chapter (**Three ways to make it happen and staying the right side of the law**), I'll give you a blueprint to embark on your own market research journey with practical steps to go from ad hoc bursts of customer discovery to building a more customer-centric business.

And finally, while I was writing this book, I asked a few of my friends, friends' kids, family and clients one simple question: *Do penguins eat peaches?* Some unexpected answers. Exactly how I like it.

Why me?

This book is the result of my own personal and professional experience and training over the last 20 years, in big and small businesses. I have supported and guided charities, solopreneurs, product and service businesses, airports, schools and big-budget FTSE 100 companies. My roles have been delightfully varied. I've worked as a journalist on the hunt for the next story. As an editor questioning everything. As a manager and leader of eclectic teams. As a product director building million-pound products. And now as a business of one, supporting other businesses to do better by their customers.

But equally, beyond business, as a friend, daughter, sister, aunt, mother and partner.

After all, what I've learnt is this: understanding customers is understanding people.

1 I made the front page of *The Sunday Times* and failed, and seven ways market research will improve your business

I made *The Sunday Times* front page.[1] Well, the money section but still… Our family gap year's finances dissected for the world to see. I had grand plans to launch a travel course to teach people how it's done.

I spent months writing content and organizing sections and I even roped in some fellow family travellers we'd met along the way. For extra credibility and all that.

I bagged myself a quasi-front-page splash in *The Sunday Times*. Then I bullishly started pre-orders. NOT ONE SALE.

COVID-19 saved me…

---

[1] K. Binns, 'We took the kids on a world tour and it was cheaper than living in Britain' in *The Sunday Times* (August 2019). Available from https://www.worldfamilytrip.com/blog/2019/8/12/travelling-the-world-was-cheaper-than-our-life-in-london

We love our own ideas. The more effort we put into them, the harder it is to turn back. Change course. Stop. It's called the sunk cost fallacy. We mix up effort and outcomes, as if the endeavour itself will define the success. Not always.

Hold your business ideas lightly. Create some healthy distance and do your homework. Listen to customers. There won't always be a global pandemic to force your hand. I got lucky.

Extract from Jungle Juice, 7th February 2022

In this opening chapter, I'll show you why you are not your customer (so stop thinking *for* them) and how making assumptions about what they want rarely ends well (personal failure coming up). I'll tell you how to spot and overcome the sunk cost fallacy (when you keep going even when you should stop) and why understanding customers is a *practice*, something you can learn and get better at. This first chapter also lays out seven ways market research will improve your business now, from testing new business ideas to improving what you already have.

You are not your customer

Let's get one thing straight. You may well have started your business scratching your own itch. Launched a vegan cheese because you couldn't find one that didn't taste like soft plastic. Opened a high-end thrift store, tired of shrunken Primark t-shirts being sold for a fiver. Or launched a coaching business following a transformational coaching experience of your own. This does not entitle you to be your customer know-it-all. Scratching your own itch can do loads of other useful things, like make it easy to connect with your first customers and help build some decent assumptions about what they could want and like. But don't mistake that for actually knowing what your customers want.

It's THE biggest mistake I see businesses make. *I know my customer, they're just like me.* Until they're not. And it all ends in tears. The moment you step into entrepreneurship, your perception of what your customers want inevitably shifts, however much you had in common with them in the early days. You are just too invested in the outcome. Your friends and family, ditto. They aren't a proxy for your customers either. They could end up being some of your first customers. But don't kid yourself, they're just being nice.

Your customers are real people. They're out there in the real world, living their messy, imperfect lives. If you want people to buy your stuff, you need to find them, talk to them so you can understand them better. As American entrepreneur Steve Blank most famously wrote (repeatedly!) in his book *The Startup Owner's Manual*: 'You need to get out of the building.'[2] Steve is something of a superstar in the start-up world. His rallying cry for businesses to go talk to customers is a simple, yet powerful, reminder of what truly matters. 'Facts exist outside the building, where future customers live and work,' he says.[3]

Talking to real people is the most effective and powerful way to understand the people you serve. To understand the context in which they live, need and use your stuff. Is it uncomfortable? Sometimes. Can you get used to it? Absolutely. Can I teach you how? Hell, yes (we'll spend quality time on this topic in Chapters 4 and 5).

Assumptions kill dreams

If we're not getting out of the building (or our home office) to find customers to talk to then how are we making our business

---

[2] S. Blank and B. Dorf, *The Startup Owners' Manual*, Wiley (March 2020).

[3] S. Blank and B. Dorf, *The Startup Owners' Manual*, Wiley (March 2020).

decisions? Assumptions. But in business, when we assume, we take a risk, a punt on something that may not be true. We do it because, often, it seems easier. We don't waste any time checking or finding out. We jump into the doing, the building, the designing, the creating and the launching. We also do it because we often fail to recognize them as such. Assumptions take hold like limpets on a rock. So tight we struggle to make out what's checked and true, and what's not.

An assumption is 'a belief or feeling that something is true or that something will happen, although there is no proof.'[4] Read those last two words out loud. *No proof.* Sounds absurd that we'd be making our way through business, betting on things turning out ok. I call it the fingers crossed strategy when we make decisions with little to no evidence. Don't get me wrong, assumptions in business *can* be useful. They have foundations. They're built on our perception of reality as *we* see it and on how *we* experience the world. They are a great starting point and can evolve into hypotheses to prove or disprove. But they need to be checked. Especially the BIG assumptions. The ones that carry the most risk in terms of time, money and precious energy.

Why are assumptions so appealing? Well, as humans, we can't sense-check everything. Our brains would implode. We assume the sun will rise in the morning. That our kids will come home safely from school. That our partner (or our pet) will still be lying next to us the next day. That our car will start. That the world won't end next Sunday. Our brain is wired to look for shortcuts. In her book, *What Your Customers Want and Can't Tell You*, Melina Palmer explains that our brains have two systems (an idea originally developed by Nobel Prize winning behavioural economist Daniel Kahneman). System 1, which she calls the *subconscious* brain, is the automatic system. 'It's quick

---

4 Oxford Learners Dictionaries' definition. Available from: www. oxfordlearnersdictionaries.com/definition/english/assumption?q= assumption

to react and can handle an incredible amount of information at any given time – to put it in computer terms as much as 11 million bits of information per second,' Melina says.[5] System 2, on the other hand, is what she calls the *conscious* brain. It's slower, more thorough (only the really important stuff makes it to this level) and can't handle as much information. Forty-five bits per second in comparison.

Melina says that far from being in control of our brains, 99% of our decisions are made by our subconscious brain (system 1), which uses proven rules, learnt behaviours and past experiences to make quick, automatic decisions. The perfect breeding ground for bias and assumptions.

Managing assumptions is also another way of managing risks. The risk of the sun not rising is tiny, so we don't check. The risk of dying in a plane crash is small, so we take that plane. The risk of the world ending on Sunday is infinitesimal, so we don't even give it a second thought. What we are doing is assessing the risk of being wrong. If it's small enough, we don't bother checking. Seriously, a smart way to live.

In business though, things aren't as simple. We glorify risk-takers and idolize rock-star entrepreneurs. *Just Do It* has become our modern slogan. But let's not confuse being comfortable taking risks with letting assumptions alone guide our every business decision. Business is not a zero-risk game and however much research you do, you can't eliminate all risks. But the successful businesses and entrepreneurs pick out their riskiest assumptions and check them. They hang out in the conscious part (system 2) of their brain for the important stuff. We're just rarely shown that side of the story.

Big businesses get caught out too. Founders and CEOs fall in love with their own idea and fail to check their biggest

[5] M. Palmer, *What Your Customer Wants and Can't Tell You: Unlocking Consumer Decisions with the Science of Behavioural Economics*, Mango, p. 23 (July 2021).

assumptions. Two well-documented public flops spring to mind. We're not used to seeing tech giants get it wrong, but in 2012 Google did just that. The search giant launched its wearables, Google Glass. Google Glass was an innovative piece of tech kit, but in 2012 nobody cared. It was a pair of glasses connected to the internet that allowed users to check messages, browse the internet and view photos. All voice and motion controlled. Groovy. Tech nerds were excited, and the Google Glass launch was out of this world (look it up). *Times Magazine* named it one of the top inventions of the year and it got a 12-page spread in *Vogue*. And still, it flopped. The need just wasn't there. At just under $2k a pair and with smart phones already widely in circulation, Google Glass was an expensive nice-to-have. Kelly Wright, Associate Account Director at Purple Agency wrote in her article, 'Four product launch failures and what we can learn from them'[6]: 'The main issue was an audience who didn't actually need or want the product. Google neglected to properly research and define their audience, assuming the hype would be enough to appeal to a generic wide audience.'

Another invention that never really took off as intended was the Segway (those weird things on two wheels). Although no longer in production, you can still spot them out in the wild (tourist hot spots and warehouses). Erika Hall is a design consultant, author and founder of service design agency Mule. In her book, *Just Enough Research*, she writes:

> Even those who could afford it [Segway] weren't sure what to do with it. You couldn't take the kids to school on it. You couldn't commute 20 miles on it. You couldn't pack the family into it or make out in its

---

[6] K. Wright, *Four product launch failures and what we can learn from them*, Purple Agency (April 2021). Available from: https://purple. agency/thoughts/four-product-launch-failures-and-what-we-can-learn-from-them

back seat… Early adopters often put up with cost and ridicule for innovations that meet real needs. But no one needs a Segway.[7]

Even the big guns get it wrong and launch things nobody wants. But bigger companies can financially cushion their flops. As a small business owner, you have more to lose heading too far down the wrong path. Sometimes so far down you can't bear the thought of turning back. It's a pretty common human trait (if that makes you feel any better) and it has a name: the sunk cost fallacy.

The sunk cost fallacy

The sunk cost fallacy inevitably follows the assumption phase. When we continue to move through our businesses on assumptions alone, things get messy. It's not because you've poured your heart and soul into something that it will work. Yes, hard work is important and enjoying that hard work (most of the time) is important, too. It will get you places. Being passionate? Equally. But in business, investing time, money and energy into something doesn't guarantee success. Effort isn't always rewarded. Unless it's guided effort. Guided by evidence of your customers' wants and needs.

Folks at the research and innovation agency, The Decision Lab, describe the sunk cost fallacy as 'a tendency to follow through on an endeavour if we have already invested time, effort or money into it, whether or not the current costs outweigh the benefits in the long run.'[8]

---

[7] E. Hall, *Just Enough Research* (2nd edition), A Book Apart, p. 2 (2019).

[8] The Decision Lab, *Why are we likely to continue with an investment even if it would be rational to give up?*, The Decision Lab. Available from: https://thedecisionlab.com/biases/the-sunk-cost-fallacy

Why do we do it? Because we're humans who experience emotions that often cause us to deviate from rational decisions. More from The Decision Lab:

> Abandoning an endeavour after committing to it and investing resources into it is likely to cause negative feelings of guilt and wastefulness. Since we want to avoid negative feelings of loss, we are likely to follow through on a decision that we have invested in even if it is not in our best interest.[9]

I know this first-hand.

(Personal) failure alert

In 2018/2019, I travelled the world for just under a year with my partner and two kids. Did it make me an expert in family travel? More than most. Did it make my family travel course a guaranteed success? No. I made assumptions. On our return, I'd decided to create an online course to help people plan a family gap year with kids. As you can appreciate, travelling with your partner, a toddler and a nine-year-old is thrilling and hard. Lots of things go well and lots of things go wrong. My course was going to prepare other families by giving them real advice on how to navigate such a life-changing adventure. I put the course on pre-order a few months before launch. I didn't make one sale.

My travel course needed to work. I'd quit my corporate job in the run-up to our trip, and back in the UK, I was still finding my feet. I'd invested time and energy in my idea. And as I mentioned in the opening lines of this chapter, I'd even secured some juicy press coverage. I'd marched so far

---

[9] The Decision Lab, *Why are we likely to continue with an investment even if it would be rational to give up?*, The Decision Lab. Available from: https://thedecisionlab.com/biases/the-sunk-cost-fallacy

down the road without properly testing my idea, assuming my target audience was just like me. I'd only consulted friends and family. But I'd already written up most of the course and it felt too late to turn back.

COVID-19 (and the subsequent ban on international travel) stopped my travel course idea in its tracks. Otherwise, who knows how far I'd have gone… I personally should have known better. I'd tested million-pound products with customers. I'd done the training and read all the books. Practised and preached, talked the talk, and walked the walk. But it was for other people's businesses. When it's your own, it's so easy to lose perspective. It doesn't just happen in business. We do it all the time. Ever started a book only to realize you're not enjoying it that much (not this one I hope!) but just kept on reading?

The sunk cost fallacy can only be avoided with a generous dose of self-awareness. We won't always dodge it (emotions are powerful things). But we can give ourselves a decent chance by checking our assumptions much earlier. Realizing you've picked the wrong path needn't be a catastrophic event. There's nothing wrong with throwing in the towel. That's bravery right there. Getting it wrong and failing is learning after all. But let's fail fast, before it's too late.

Knowing your customer is a practice

So far, you've learnt that you're not your customer, that assumptions are dangerous, and investments in terms of time, energy and money won't guarantee success. What do we do next? Well, we check. We find out. We test. We discover and we question. Not just the once but as we go along because things change. Customers are people and people change. Trends come and go and global pandemics uplift foundations we thought unbreakable in our modern societies. Customers are a moving target so we can't be complacent. We need to pay attention. Successful brands do just that. They evolve, innovate and move with the times. They use customer research as a tool to understand their audience and make changes when necessary.

Let me introduce you to Dr Lennart Nacke. He teaches User Experience (UX) Gamification at the University of Waterloo in Toronto, Canada. 'Good business strategy is fuelled by user research,' Lennart told me in an interview. He shared an example from the toy giant Lego and how it turned some of its then financial woes around by going back to its core users: kids.

In the 1980s and 1990s, Lego was diversifying its offering big time. Building amusement parks, launching video games and exploring all sorts of franchise tie-ins. As for its playsets, the Lego City line was its most significant product. Kids could build city-inspired projects like trains and police stations and play cops and robbers with matching mini figures. The Lego City product generated about 30% of the entire company's revenue in 1999. 'That dropped to about 3% over the next few years,' Lennart explained. This was happening because they were mainly building specialized sets, which included specialized pieces that were more expensive to produce than standard Lego bricks.

Jørgen Vig Knudstorp took the helm of the company in the early 2000s when Lego was allegedly losing $1million a day. Creating special Lego set pieces was costly and overall sales were falling. The new CEO turned to research and called in a bunch of anthropologists to observe and study kids at play. 'Those anthropologists went in and did testing with kids. They listened to kids. Watched kids play. Gradually, they started to understand that kids are really telling stories with their toys,' Lennart said.

Through these interviews and observations, they got a better and deeper understanding of the meaning of play to kids. The research helped Lego understand how the bricks fitted into kids' storytelling. The researchers learnt that kids were already creating stories about firefighters and police officers. Lego needed to focus on the stories these kids were creating and allow kids to combine the basic (and cheaper to make) blocks instead of new blocks and sets.

The findings led to changes, including improving manufacturing cost and efficiency, reducing the number of specialized bricks per playset, and selling off or franchising periphery businesses. And it worked. 'It turned things around. This type of work can have a financial impact,' Lennart said.

Market research, as a regular practice, is not always the norm for smaller businesses. Many freelancers, consultants and small independent businesses I work with get tongue-tied when I question them about their customers. I sense a glimpse of guilt and a shadow of shame for not knowing enough. Making the decision to be self-employed or set up a business is unfortunately not like buying your first house or renting your first home. No one hands you a bunch of keys that unlock all the doors.

Understanding customers is not a given or something businesses can take for granted. It's a practice. A never-ending loop of discovery. Sometimes we'll lean on it more than other times and that's fine. Sometimes we'll do it imperfectly and that's fine too. We can never know everything there is to know about our customers, but we need to at least try to find out the important stuff.

Seven ways market research will improve your business

Don't spend another penny on fancy logos, elaborate websites, branding, marketing and content strategists before finding out whether people *actually* want what you're selling. It's like hiring a celebrity chef and paying them to teach you how to cook a gourmet meal. You source a bunch of fancy ingredients, but you realize all your pots have holes in them. It doesn't matter how good the food could've looked, how good the food could've tasted, there is no food if you're cooking from a leaky pot. In the kitchen, as in business, you need to have your basics in place. Consider market research as a key business basic. Your Le Creuset pot if you like. It's the foundation on which everything else should be built. Market research *will* improve your business. Fact. Here are seven ways market research can improve yours:

- Find your audience
- Power up your marketing
- Generate new ideas
- Test a new business idea
- Improve something
- Tackle unconscious bias
- Make money, find money

Let's go through them one by one.

1. Find your audience: who are my customers?

Unless you're Amazon, your product or service is not for everyone. Seriously, ask yourself: *Who is my customer? What do I know about them? How do I know it's true?* Whether you have a business or aspire to set one up, finding your crowd is half the battle. And the more laser focused you are on who you're after, the more chances you have of creating something they want and buy. Don't be for everyone. In other words, find a *niche*.

Whether you're on the hunt for your first paying customers or want to ensure you continue to have customers who pay, market research helps you keep things tight. You'd normally start with assumptions. If you're selling premium organic baby clothes online, you'd assume your customers are parents with babies. You might even assume that mums tend to do most of the baby clothes buying. So, you define your audience as 'mums of babies'. You dig a little deeper into the purchases you've had so far, set up a few customer calls (Chapter 4 will show you how to find people to talk to) only to realize that over a third of your sales come from grandparents, another third from mums of babies and the final third come from women who don't have kids at all.

After a bit more digging you realize your brand is regarded as gifting material by friends and family (of parents with babies). In fact, you realize that most of the baby mums who you thought were your main customers have quickly cottoned on to the fact that spending £50 on an organic babygrow doesn't make economic sense in the long run (babies are pooping, vomiting, fast-growing little machines). But they don't half make a lovely gift when others are paying.

Armed with this new insight you start getting your products on gift guides. You partner with some baby shower planners. You start putting some serious effort into marketing during gifting seasons and you hunt down the baby boomers happy to splurge on their new grandkids. And there you have it... you realize your customers were *not* a monolith block of trendy, eco-conscious mums after all.

Market research also helps you identify other people involved in your customer's decision to buy (or not). Think about it, when you buy a brand-new sofa do you buy it without talking about it to anyone? If you hire a childminder, will you choose someone without consulting the other caregiver? If you're in a relationship, you probably discuss important purchases before getting the credit card out.

I remember the day I hired Emma George without running it past my partner first (ask for forgiveness not permission and all that...). Emma runs the professional home organizing business Home Organise with Emma. I waited until the day before she was booked to arrive to tell my partner a stranger was coming into the house to help me declutter and organize our bedroom. He was unimpressed with my tardy ways to say the least (until he saw the result). How many other partners *did* discuss getting a home organizer and were met with resistance? If Emma knew this, she could start addressing that resistance head on. Unpick it and create content or FAQs that could quell some of those fears about strangers rummaging in your underwear drawer (I promise, they don't).

So don't forget the others: the influencers and the budget holders. Customers rarely exist in a vacuum.

I run the following exercise in my signature Customer Clarity workshop. You'll find it useful to get you started too. I bet you'll be genuinely surprised at just how much of what you think you know about your audience has in fact never been checked.

Permission to just skip on by and keep reading (judgement-free zone here). This exercise will still be here when you're in the mood, have the time, or ideally both.

Stretch task #1[*]

- Get a piece of paper, blank Word document, or notes/voice app.

- Set timer for 15 minutes.

- Write down your current key target customers (e.g. 40+ women, Gen Z, cyclists, etc).

- For each target group, write down everything you (think) you know about them (think demographics but also behaviours).

- Go through the assumptions one by one and ask yourself: *Is this true? How do I know?* And identify the ones that need checking.

- Save all unchecked assumptions. You'll need them when you start talking to customers (coming up in Chapters 4 and 5).

*All stretch tasks can be downloaded from www.productjungle.co.uk/book/resources

2. Power up your marketing: am I speaking my customers' language?

Great marketing copy speaks to us directly and viscerally. Language really matters and market research helps you uncover what language matters to your audience. Have you noticed what it feels like when you read something (an email, a social media post, a brochure, an ad) that speaks to you? It moves you on some level. It makes you think this business, this brand *gets* me (I have a great toilet paper example for you coming up in Chapter 5).

Great products and services flop all the time. Not (always) because they're rubbish, but because business owners fail to articulate the value of what they have to offer in words that matter to their audience. They either can't find the words or are convinced they're using the right ones without double-checking with customers.

Words can be a barrier to people choosing your product over someone else's. My own business Product Jungle® is a case in point. When I set up my consultancy my head was still stuck in the corporate world. I wanted to offer product management services to small businesses – extract the useful bits from that corporate discipline. Nobody was listening. They didn't get it. My first business book pitch was very similar to the book you have in your hands today, but the words 'market research' weren't even mentioned. Instead, I talked about concepts such as test and learn and agile research. In return, I got mainly glazed eyes and polite nods.

It's only after launching into another lengthy explanation (always a bad sign) of what Product Jungle® actually did that someone interrupted me and said: 'So, you do market research then?'

Market research. I resisted the term itself for a LONG time. Not my smartest move.

The terms I could get behind were customer discovery, customer research, UX and product management. But then I remembered that it was never about me. Even if you are a bona fide expert or you started out as your own ideal customer, as soon as you're running the show you've removed yourself one level of understanding. You need to check.

A few signs your language might not be landing with your target audience:

- You find yourself overexplaining what you do. This normally means you aren't 100% sure how to describe what you do either.
- Your audience is confused. You get too much polite digital nodding but not enough engagement.
- You're out of synch with customer perceptions. Your audience sees you one way. Just not quite the way you want.
- You get lots of high-level interest but no actual sales.

Dana Publicover is managing director of Publicover, her eponymous agency that helps businesses attract and convert the right customers. She told me:

> When your language isn't working, your customers aren't saying *this language isn't working for me*. They just stop buying… If you're getting a lot of traffic, a lot of visitors, a lot of interest but that interest isn't converting into long-term repeat customer relationships, that's a classic symptom of a communication challenge.

It happens to the best of us. It happens when you start, when you launch a new product and when you are trying to revive an existing one. Customer language is something you need to keep on top of. Give this a try… Once again, you have a permission slip to keep reading and to come back to this task.

Stretch task #2

- Pick three people in your target audience.

- Ask them to describe what you do (if they're already aware of you) or ask them to look at your website/socials and then describe to you what you do, and what you have to offer.

- Keep your questions neutral. For example: *How would you describe this?* or *What do you think this means?*

- Identify gaps. Explore language. Close gaps.

As Dana explained to me:

> Your customers have all the information you need. You just have to ask them for it. You need to talk to people who buy, who don't buy, and people who you hope will buy. By talking to them, you're going to learn their language. It's like suddenly becoming vegan or starting CrossFit, there's a lingo, a language that you learn, a vocabulary. You need to figure out what vocabulary your customers use.

Dana shared an example of a client of hers in the wellness space:

> My client was positioning her services as a wellness thing. We realized that, in fact, the concept of wellness was too woo for the clients she was targeting. Her offer was much more practical – yoga and meditation on demand. We asked her target customers, *What is wellness?* And they all explained the things she is not.

A classic example of a mismatch between the language you use and how your customers perceive it.

Sometimes, we're so scared of alienating certain audiences (because we think we're Amazon and our offer is for everyone), we word large. In Dana's client's case, wellness was the *large* concept or what we call the highest common denominator. The safe and deceivingly obvious option, perhaps. But sometimes the wrong words turn people away. In business, if you want people to join in, to follow and to buy, don't let words be a barrier. Speak to people. Listen gently and with curiosity. What's in a word? Everything. Choose wisely.

3. Generate new ideas: what can I do next?

Talking to your people, even when you don't feel like it, is tonic for your (business) soul. It's a bit like a friend telling you to go for a jog when you're feeling low. You know it'll help but the first step is the hardest. If you're in a business funk, unsure what to do next, talk to customers. Doing market research is not just for when you have an idea. It's also brilliant when you don't have a clue (it's fine not to always know what the hell you're supposed to be doing next by the way). Just don't stay clueless for too long. Speaking to your target audience, asking good questions and listening without any specific goal in mind is the best way to dig yourself out of a hole. I guarantee that even a few customer conversations (we'll look at how to set them up and what to ask in Chapters 4 and 5) will get your business brain buzzing again.

Let me introduce you to a former client, Lara Sheldrake. Lara is the founder of Found & Flourish, an online community for female-owned businesses. In 2022, she felt lost. 'I had researched what to ask and how, via various resources online, but the data I had collected from my customer research was throwing so many inconclusive answers, I began questioning everything. This uncertainty left me feeling pretty helpless,' she told me.

After a call to probe a bit deeper into Lara's uncertainties, I developed a discussion guide with some high-level questions around key topic areas, relevant to the community she'd created:

I followed Katie's suggestions and once I knew what questions I should be asking, within a matter of weeks I had connected with my audience on a far deeper level than I knew was even possible. I finally had the clarity and confidence I needed to rewrite my business strategy based on what my audience actually wanted and needed. I relaunched our business offering after making the necessary changes and the response was better than anything I could have imagined!

Powerful stuff.

Lara made changes to her offering following her interviews with members, including paring down the online resource provision, creating more in-real-life opportunities for members to connect and collaborate as well as reducing the number of newsletters Found & Flourish was sending out.

If you don't have a pro by your side (see ways to work with me at the end of this book), *Do Penguins Eat Peaches?* is the next best thing. By the end of this book, you too will be able to find people to speak to (Chapter 4), craft the right questions (Chapter 5), and make sense of what you've learnt (Chapter 6). DIY market research at its best. So, like moving your butt off the sofa when you're feeling blue, talking to customers when your business brain is flatlining works. As Stephen Wunker, Jessica Wattman and David Farber remind us in their book *Jobs to Be Done*: 'The customer is always right. Especially when it comes to innovation. Whether they know it or not, customers have the answers for where the next big breakthrough will be.'[10]

4. Test a new business idea: will this work?

Market research is the obvious place to start when it comes to new. New business, new product and new service. And that's

---

[10] S. Wunker, J. Wattman and D. Farber, *Jobs to Be Done: A Roadmap for Customer-Centred Innovation*, AMACOM, p. 3 (2017).

probably the one area where you know it's needed. Sometimes we launch something new when enough customers ask for it (please can you make this jumper in green). Great. But sometimes (in fact quite often) you have an idea, a hunch and need to find out whether it's a goer.

You can become self-employed or set up a business with very little administrative effort these days. It doesn't mean it'll work out for you. People need to be buying your stuff. Doing online market research (what we'll call secondary research) is usually a good place to start. Some of you may well have skim read trend reports, headed to your local library (old-school) or joined a business community for an answer to that critical question: *Will people buy?* But secondary research (lots more to come on this topic in Chapter 8) is only part of your discovery journey. Asking target customers directly (primary research) will give you the best insight into whether your idea has wings. And believe me, it's not just about asking potential customers whether they *like* your idea, as you'll learn later (Chapter 5 will teach you how to ask quality questions).

In Erika Hall's *Just Enough Research*, she warns us that likability is a misleading measure:

> As you start interviewing people… you might refer to what they do or don't like. *Like* is not part of the critical thinker's vocabulary. On some level, we all want things we do to be liked, so it's easy to treat likability as a leading success indicator. But the concept of 'liking' is as subjective as it is empty… This means you can't get any useful insights from any given individual reporting that they *like* or *hate* a particular thing. I like horses, but I'm not going to buy any online.[11]

---

[11] E. Hall, *Just Enough Research* (2nd edition), A Book Apart, p. 7 (2019).

Before we move on. Remember, friends' and family's opinions don't count as evidence either. They'll either be your cheerleaders or your naysayers. Either way, don't rely on them to tell you whether your idea will sell or not.

5. Improve something: can I do this better?

Market research isn't just for shiny and new either. It's a great way to get inspiration to improve what you already offer. There's nearly always an opportunity to get better. The trick is not to always ask customers outright how you can improve (learn to be a feedback pro in Chapter 10). Start by asking them to talk you through why, how and when they use your current product or service. Note where customers are taking shortcuts or using your product or service in a way that you didn't expect, and explore what other products and services they use to satisfy the same need.

Let's take a fictional example. Ade creates online social media courses for independent, creative product makers. Her courses are video based. She's making sales but not getting much feedback and wants to explore how she can improve her offer. She starts looking at the usage data on her course hosting platform. She notices that while people are buying her courses, they aren't completing them and, in some cases, they're not even starting them. Armed with this insight, Ade sets up five calls with some of her previous customers. She asks about when they bought her course, why they bought it, and how, more generally, they go about learning new business skills. She also asks them to talk her through their typical day. Ade learns that many makers spend most of their working time in the studio (or in the kitchen) making their products. The rest of the time, they're packing up orders or visiting suppliers. In other words, they're always on the go. She quickly realizes that her video-based courses don't easily slot into creative makers' lives. She asks about where else they seek out small business advice and they all mention podcasts as they can listen while doing. Ade trials her next course using exclusively audio. It's an instant hit with her audience and takes her less time to produce. Win. Win.

When thinking of ways to better your offer, don't start by asking your customers outright *How can I improve?* By all means, you can ask this question at the end of a conversation, as you might capture something of interest. But as you can see from Ade's example, there are more interesting questions to ask that will help you innovate. We'll be diving deep into the best questions to ask customers in Chapter 5.

6. Tackle unconscious bias

Humans are biased. Humans set up businesses, therefore businesses are biased. Fact. Market research, the act of intentionally seeking to understand others (our customers), can keep our biases in check. In research, biases are well defined. From confirmation bias (the tendency to unconsciously look for and give more weight to data, feedback and behaviours that confirm our existing assumptions) to false consensus bias (the tendency to assume that everyone thinks and behaves like us), market research gives us the language to spot, acknowledge and tackle bias head on. What you can name, you can change.

Trina Moore Pervall is a UX researcher and designer. In an article for *Smashing Magazine*, she writes about the role designers and researchers play when it comes to dismantling bias:

> As designers, we want to design optimal experiences for the diverse range of people a product will serve. To achieve this, we take steps in our research and design decisions to minimize the risk of alienating product-relevant social identities, including but not limited

to disability, race/ethnicity, gender, skin colour, age, sexual orientation and language.[12]

If the world has taught us anything these last few years, it is that we need to get better at recognizing the big uncomfortable unconscious biases that exist within each of us. Racism. Sexism. Classism. Ageism. Ableism. These biases trickle through into business decisions like sticky treacle. As Melina Palmer writes:

> People often aspire to have a completely unbiased perspective. When it comes to the human brain, it is important to know that none of us can be without bias. Ever. The subconscious brain's rules of thumb are based on past experiences and biases. They are always there. While you can't eliminate them, understanding them makes things a whole lot smoother.[13]

Beyond a moral responsibility, inclusivity (which emerges as a result of acknowledging and tackling our biases) makes economic sense for businesses. Lydia Amoah is author of *The Black Pound Report*, the only in-depth study of multi-ethnic consumer spending in the UK. Ethnic minority spending is grossly underestimated due to persistent bias and stereotypes. Lydia's research reveals the average total monthly disposable income of multi-ethnic consumers in the UK is £375 million. That's £4.5 billion per year. 'This makes it one of the world's

---

[12] T. Moore-Pervall, *Unconscious bias that gets in the way of inclusive design*, Smashing Magazine (September 2022). Available from: www.smashingmagazine.com/2022/09/unconscious-biases-inclusive-design

[13] M. Palmer, *What Your Customer Wants and Can't Tell You: Unlocking Consumer Decisions with the Science of Behavioural Economics*, Mango, p. 42 (July 2021).

most exciting and untapped audiences,' Lydia explains.[14] In the UK, Black, Asian and multi-ethnic consumers make up 16% of the population, a majority of whom don't feel catered for by major retailers, according to Lydia's findings. The fact it took Johnson & Johnson one hundred years to redesign their plasters to cater for darker skin tones is a case in point.

Groups are crying out for more inclusive experiences. And they have money to spend. Clare Seal is a money expert and author. She also has ADHD. In a post on her Instagram account, Clare called on banks to think more about neurodiversity when it comes to financial services:

> Finding the systems for managing your money when you have ADHD is really HARD. Having ADHD is expensive, it makes emotional connection to money even more fraught and intensifies the shame we feel about mistakes that we've made in our financial lives. We're not 'bad with money' – we're frustrated with the systems that make it difficult for us to manage it successfully.[15]

This isn't a problem neurotypical people are going to solve. She adds:

> We need big banks to put their money where their mouth is and invest in creating tools and services that are compatible with neurodivergent brains, and inclusive to those who think differently. We need

---

[14] L. Amoah, *The Black Pound Report 2022: A study of the multi-ethnic consumer*, backlight.uk. Available from: www.backlight.uk/black-pound-report

[15] C. Seal @myfrugalyear, Instagram (November 2022). Available from: www.instagram.com/p/CljaVwyMExy

funded research into what will really help us to break down some of our barriers to financial wellbeing.

Big brands are broadly moving in the right direction when it comes to inclusivity (whether it's from a place of morality, future profit or both remains to be seen). But while the direction of travel is clear, the pace is painfully slow. Small businesses can be part of that change too. We may not be trained UX designers, but we have an opportunity, through market research, to tackle unconscious bias head on. And our size makes us nimbler and faster to react.

We won't always get it right. That's part of the messy, uncomfortable journey of waking up to the fact that not everyone is like us. But we have a duty to try and to keep trying. Whether it's age, race, sex, gender, ability or neurodiversity, market research exposes our blind spots. So, don't stay stuck in your comfort zone. Go talk to people who are not like you, who don't talk like you and who don't look like you. There's an opportunity for small businesses to attract and serve new audiences, to do the right thing, and to make a profit. It's less about equality of experiences (same experience for everyone) and more about equity (acknowledging that people come with unique circumstances that require more tailored experiences). Even your own customer base is almost certainly less monolith than you think.

7. Make money, find money

At the end of the day, if people don't buy your stuff or use your services, your business won't survive. Unless you're already filthy rich (good for you), you need sales to make a living. *Making a living* means different things to different people. Maybe you want to pay yourself a salary, hire people to help or be able to take more time off. If you are completely self-funded, those early months and years may be tough with lots of decisions to make. The best decisions will always be those based on evidence. Those are the ones that will help you reach your financial business goals faster.

Ultimately it comes down to maths. And in some cases, the numbers just don't add up. You may be confident you have a product or service people want (because you've checked). It's selling but you're not hitting your financial goals. The problem could be a pricing (hold tight for lots of pricing tips in Chapter 11) or a volume issue, as in you need to sell more.

You may be at a stage when you're seeking investment for your business. In that case, you'll need to show evidence you understand your target customer. Potential investors will want to see you've taken the time to talk to people in your target market, to ask them the right questions and that you've read all the latest trend reports. Doing this right will give you a better chance of securing the cash you need. It makes sense. Would you hand over money to a business without evidence it has customers willing to buy?

Spending time understanding the people you are trying to serve helps make all the numbers add up.

To sum up

Essentially, market research helps businesses find their audience, speak their language, pull them out of a funk, test new ideas, improve their offer, tackle biases and ultimately make more money. It's all about confident decision making. I'm certainly not advocating creating an evidence file for every single decision, but market research will make the important decisions – those that define how we spend our time, energy and money, that little bit easier. Let's stop leaving that to chance. Businesses aren't for the lucky, they are for the prepared.

So why are so many of us not doing it, or doing it all wrong? In our next chapter we'll explore what holds so many of us back when it comes to market research. From excuses and an underlying fear of failure to the dangers of ego-driven decision making.

> ### Chapter 1 recap:
>
> • You are not your customer so stop guessing what they want.
>
> • Always check assumptions (ask yourself what evidence do I have to suggest this is true?).
>
> • Beware of the sunk cost fallacy (the tendency to follow through with something just because we're invested in it).
>
> • Market research helps you find your audience; improve your marketing; generate new ideas; test new products and services; improve your offer; tackle unconscious bias and make money.

2 Ego, excuses and the fear of failure: what's holding you back?

A week after attending my market research workshop, one of the participants emailed me to say she'd done some customer interviews. Brilliant, I responded. 'But my customers won't pay for my one-to-one consulting session idea,' she wrote back, disappointment oozing through her words. She ran a shop. The bricks and mortar kind with happy, loyal customers. She had her hopes on launching a one-to-one offer. But it wasn't to be. Not this time.

Talking to customers might not always turn out as planned. Brilliant. You learnt something. That idea you held a tad too tight... they may not need it (yet).

The cost of being wrong early? Bruised ego. Sure, it sucks. But think about it... No time wasted creating something nobody wants and no crushing disappointment as you launch to crickets.

Extract from Jungle Juice, 20th June 2022

I n this chapter, I'll debunk eight common excuses that stop businesses from doing market research. Here they are:

- Customers don't know what they want
- It's only for big businesses
- I already know my customer
- You can have a successful business without it
- You need to speak to hundreds of people
- It's a waste of time
- I don't know how
- Someone will copy my idea

Over the next few pages, we'll unpick them, one by one. Then we'll dive into the other powerful forces at play when it comes to not doing the work: the fear of failure and big business egos.

Market research excuses

The market research industry has its fair share of stubborn myths that so easily morph into convenient excuses not to do the work. But excuses hold you back. They comfort you in your own inaction and so often send you on the wrong path. Let's expose a few, shall we?

1. Customers don't know what they want (so there's no point asking)

When quotes are taken out of context, all sorts of misunderstandings are born. Henry Ford (1863–1947) was an American industrialist. He founded the eponymous car company Ford Motors and was widely credited for building the first mass produced car assembly line. Henry famously (and allegedly) said: 'If I'd have asked them [people] what they wanted, they would have said faster horses.' This quote is often taken out of context and used as evidence that there is little point asking customers what they want. True. Customers don't always know what they want. But they *do* know what they're trying to get done (in the case of Henry's customers, getting from A to B faster). They probably knew how they felt about existing transport methods (frustratingly slow). Could they imagine a metal box on wheels would be the answer to their transport woes? Unlikely.

It's not up to your customers to come up with innovative solutions to improve their lives. They're too busy living it. It's up to you as a business to identify their biggest problems (which need to be painful enough for them to want to pay to solve them), their delights and ultimately what they're trying to get done. Once you have a solid grasp of the problem space you can start to think of solutions. So, yes, customers don't always know what product or feature they want. When talking to customers, don't waste too much time asking them what they want you to build next. You'll get better insight asking them what they're trying to get done, by seeking to understand the context in which they use the current product/service and by exploring their emotional landscape.

This idea of figuring out what customers are trying to get done is powerful. It can be a game changer for your business. It has a name too: Jobs to Be Done (JTBD for short). For now, just remember the name. We'll come back to JTBD and the right questions to ask customers in Chapter 5.

2. It's only for big business

Yes. Big businesses spend big bucks on understanding customers. The global market research services industry was worth $81.13 billion in 2022.[1] In the UK alone, the MRS valued the sector

---

[1] The Business Research Company, *Market Research Services Global Market Report 2023*, thebusinessresearchcompany.com (January 2023). Available from: www.thebusinessresearchcompany.com/report/market-research-services-global-market-report

at £8 billion (2022).[2] That's a hell of a lot of money spent on customer research with larger businesses making up the bulk of that spend. As the competitive landscape becomes more crowded and the economic pressures more acute, larger businesses are increasingly seeking out answers to *why* their customers behave as they do.

The fundamental rules of business are, by and large, the same, however big or small you are. You have something you want to sell, and you need customers to buy it.

So, no, market research is not exclusively for big businesses. It's for you too. To reduce risk and gather evidence so you can build products and services people want and buy. Big companies have bigger teams and bigger budgets. Sure. But the bigger you grow the more effort you need to make to stay close to your customers. You get heavier, and you're slower to respond to customer changes. Big brands fear you. Small can be your superpower.

3. I already know my customer

In Chapter 1, I told you why you are not your customer. You may well be an absolute legend in your field of business. That doesn't mean you're a customer-know-it-all. You started your business solving your own problem? You are still not your customer. Both these starting points will give you a head start but don't get cosy. Customers change and evolve. Having a grasp on your customer demographics (age, gender, average income, etc.) is no longer enough.

---

[2] Market Research Society (MRS), *UK research sector worth increases to over £8billion following a 6.4% growth in 2021, MRS reveals*, mrs.org.uk (December 2022). Available from: www.mrs.org.uk/article/mrs/uk-research-sector-worth-increases-to-over-8billion-following-64-growth-in-2021-mrs-reveals-

4. You can have a successful business without it

Maybe. If you're lucky. Right time, right place, and all that. There are businesses that launched and scaled successfully without *officially* doing market research. This can happen for a few reasons. First, they tackled a really obvious customer want or need (no-brainer) and had what we call a first mover's advantage. Second, the founder was particularly good (albeit subconsciously) at understanding customers and tapping into consumer trends. Market research in anything but name. Problems tend to arise when these so-called lucky businesses launch their second product, try to scale or when their empathetic founder moves on. Because they never consciously understood why things worked so well the first time around.

5. You need to speak to hundreds of people

False. Great one to use as an excuse for not speaking to anyone. Especially when we are small and have little resources. Yes, having a large sample size when putting out a survey can be useful for high-risk business decisions. Or for governments responsible for shaping policy. But when it comes to interviewing customers, you don't need to speak to hundreds of people. There are pages and pages online about the optimum number of people to speak to. The important law at the heart of this debate is the law of diminishing returns. Research shows there is a point at which you stop learning anything new. The type of research you are doing will determine the number of people you need to speak to. Here are a few guidelines to use:

- For **surveys**, Survey Monkey has a handy sample size calculator.[3] It does all the complicated number crunching for you. More on surveys in Chapter 7.

---

[3] Survey Monkey, *Sample size calculator*, surveymonkey.co.uk. Available from: https://www.surveymonkey.co.uk/mp/sample-size-calculator

- For **usability testing** (e.g. does this website work for my audience? Does this app work as expected? Does this product function as expected?), research gurus at the Nielsen Norman Group (NN/g), a global reference in the design research world, recommend five users.[4] I know. Doesn't sound a lot, does it? But 85% of all usability issues will be flagged by speaking to five people. Five!
- For **customer interviews** (see Chapter 5 for how to find people to speak to and what to ask), recommendations vary.
  - For **small-sized businesses**, interviewing 7–12 people is usually enough. But even five real conversations will go a long way in deepening your understanding of customers.
  - If you are **targeting multiple, distinct customer groups** best practice suggests speaking to between 4–6 people per group.

6. It's a waste of time

Market research is anything but a waste of time. Yes, it takes a bit of time upfront, but the biggest waste of time is surely building stuff nobody wants. And besides, once you get stuck in, it can be fun. As Erika Hall, author of *Just Enough Research* writes: 'Unless you are naturally curious about people, research can seem like annoying homework at first. Once you get into it though, you'll find it totally fun and useful. A little knowledge opens up a whole world of new problems to solve.'[5]

---

[4] M. Rosala, *How many participants for a UX interview?*, Nielsen Norman Group (NN/g) (October 2021). Available from: www.nngroup.com/articles/interview-sample-size

[5] E. Hall, *Just Enough Research* (2nd edition), A Book Apart, p. 21 (2019).

7. I don't know how

Not knowing *how* to do market research is another real barrier for smaller businesses. It's the premise of this book. There's plenty of support out there for everything else you need to know. Marketing. Social media. Design. Branding. PR. Sales. But market research? A gaping hole in many small businesses' toolkit. Not for long folks. Keep reading.

8. Someone will copy my idea

Copycats. Our final excuse. Some of you fear that if you talk about your idea, someone will pinch it. Playing the copycat card as a reason not to do research tends to be more prevalent in competitive business landscapes. However, smaller businesses can fall prey to it too although this excuse rarely stands up to scrutiny. For starters, an idea without implementation is just an idea. Nebulous. Hopeful and probably not all that unique. And second, doing market research well is always about exploring the problem space first before testing solutions.

Beyond these common excuses, there are usually a few other (deeper) things holding us back.

Fear of failure

Another reason we don't engage in much customer research is because we fear failure. Subconsciously perhaps. What if we're wrong? What if people don't like our ideas? What if they don't buy our products? We often don't even realize fear is driving our reluctance to do the work when it comes to understanding customers. But nine times out of ten it is.

Fear has kept us safe as a species and ensured our survival. The sensations we feel when 'under threat' (or wrong) are deeply engrained in the human psyche. It's a scientific fact. It's not just you, it's all of us. We're social animals at heart. We crave connection, community, commonality and safety.

We fear being shunned by our 'tribe'. In sabre tooth tiger days, to be booted out of the cave was a dangerous and often deadly move.

Times have changed. But our brains not as much as we'd think. We avoid situations that could end up with rejection (No, I don't want to speak to you; No, I don't like your idea; No, I don't really understand what you do; You got that all wrong didn't you?). We also avoid any situation that might end up telling us that we've failed in some way. It sets off a chemical reaction in our brains that screams DANGER.

Nobody likes to be wrong. But in business, it will happen. We need to reframe failing as learning. Recognize the fear and acknowledge it as a normal human response and go find some customers to talk to and observe anyway. Learning that your idea won't work *sooner* rather than later is not failure. In business, I'd call that success. Market research is not dangerous. If you *don't* do it upfront, you might think you're avoiding failure. But, more often than not, you're heading straight for it. Business consultant and author Jonny Schneider told me: 'Like many of us, I was optimized for being right. Throughout my career I thought if I work hard, I will succeed. But sometimes you fail even when you're trying. These days, I set myself up to be wrong.'

While fear holds us back, ego comforts us in our inertia. It deceivingly whispers: there's no point checking because you're *always* right. Ego is another barrier to understanding customers.

Ego

Ego. Let's start with the modern definition. 'Ego is your sense of your own value and importance.'[6] In business, it makes us fall in love with our own ideas. Our ego is fragile. It becomes

---

[6] Oxford Leaners Dictionary's definition. Available from: www.oxfordlearnersdictionaries.com/definition/english/ego?q=ego

defensive when faced with criticism and protective when challenged. In business this manifests itself under different guises. Wanting to be right. Only listening to what we want to hear. Avoiding tough feedback. In his book, *Ego is the Enemy*, Ryan Holiday described the ego as 'an unhealthy belief in your own importance. Arrogance. Self-centred ambition.'[7]

Ego doesn't only manifest itself as a loud, brash, self-centred version of ourselves. Ego can be more subtle and quieter, although it still gets defensive and convinces us that we're right. Basically, everyone's ego will try it on. When it comes to understanding customers, ego often shows up as resistance to doing the work. The checking, the finding out and talking to customers. 'Resistance will reason with you like a lawyer or jam a nine-millimetre in your face like a stickup man,' writes Steven Pressfield in his book *Do the Work*.[8] He candidly adds: 'Resistance is always lying and full of shit.'[9] Agreed.

Ego is so crafty; it sometimes even makes us believe it's our gut doing the talking. If I got a pound for every social media post written about listening to our gut, I'd be rich. Always be aware. Is it really your gut? Or is it just your ego in disguise? So, how does our ego show up in business? And how do we distinguish it from our crafty ego talking? I find these two often get mixed up.

My gut often tells me things I don't want to hear but are true:

- This working rhythm is unsustainable, you're going to burn out.
- You might want to check whether it's worth it before you plough all your time and energy into that idea.
- You really need to spend more one-on-one time with your son.

---

[7] R. Holiday, *Ego is the Enemy*, Profile Books (2016).

[8] S. Pressfield, *Do the Work*, Black Irish Entertainment, p. 6 (2011).

[9] S. Pressfield, *Do the Work*, Black Irish Entertainment, p. 7 (2011).

My ego on the other hand tells me:

- You're working hard towards your goals; it's supposed to be all consuming. Keep going!
- Just do it, launch the damn thing already.
- Ah don't worry teenagers don't want to spend time with their mums anyway.

Not listening to customers, not taking time to really understand them and their needs, is a bit like ignoring your gut and letting ego be the loudest voice in the room.

We need to keep our egos in check every step of our customer discovery journey. Because ego surfaces even once we've done the work. We've got the feedback; we've reviewed the survey responses and we've spoken to customers. But then if we're not careful, we slip into selective listening mode. Your ego blocks out what you don't want to hear. Be alert.

Stretch task #3

Do you find yourself getting defensive quickly? Are you aware (awareness is the first step to change, folks) that you like being right a bit TOO much? If so, this is a great stretch task for you.

Practise being wrong. Sounds simplistic? It's anything but. Practise with your partner, your friends, your kids, your dog and your parents. It will sting. You'll be swallowing pride for pudding. But you'll survive. Here are a few useful words to get you started:

- Do you know what? You might be right…

- I might be mistaken you know…

- You're right, I got it wrong this time…

To sum up

As we have seen in this chapter, lots of things get in the way of understanding customers: excuses that will immobilize you like quicksand. But also, the more subtle forces at play. The quiet voices reminding us that if we check, if we ask questions, we may well be wrong. We may fail. Alongside failure, this chapter also exposed how our egos happily attempt to derail us. So, what lies beyond excuses, egos and fear when it comes to business? Three simple qualities: curiosity, empathy and courage. In the next chapter, we look at how to reframe these sometimes-nebulous qualities as tools and use them to your advantage.

Chapter 2 recap:

- Excuses are powerful immobilizers when it comes to understanding customers. Spot them before they stop you.

- Everyone is scared (of getting it wrong, of rejection, of failure).

- Your ego will try it on. Every time.

- Practise being wrong.

3 The explorer's toolkit: curiosity, empathy and courage

I was eight months pregnant with my second. In a swimsuit in Sardinia. Whale-like (nope there's no photo). She was svelte, sporty, well-groomed and vaguely familiar. 'I'm taking a well-deserved break,' she told me as our sons played together in the resort grounds.

I need one too, I thought. 'It's been SO busy these past few months,' she insisted. Whatever, I thought. My second pregnancy nearly killed me, literally. My natural curiosity? All dried up. So, I just sat there. Sipping mocktails.

First week back. I slump onto the sofa and turn on the news. It was election night. 'OMG that's her,' I said. THE British political journalist. THE really famous one. The questions I'd have asked... If only I knew.

You don't know what you don't know. Go back and read that again. That's the beauty of talking to customers. You spot the magic you didn't even know existed. But you have to be CURIOUS (unless you're heavily pregnant then all is forgiven).

Extract from Jungle Juice, 11ᵗʰ April 2022

Being an explorer in business means approaching things with a beginner's mind. It's that feeling you get when you step off a plane in a brand-new city, when you try a new hobby for the very first time or when you find yourself in a room full of strangers. Approach customer understanding in the same way: with curiosity, empathy and a healthy dose of courage. You might not consider these qualities as tools in the traditional sense but redefining them as such helps you apply them in business more efficiently. As tools, curiosity, empathy and courage move out of the nebulous realm of emotional to the realm of practicality. In this chapter, I'll show you essentially how to channel your inner five-year-old (we were all curious once) and what you need to build your explorer's toolkit.

Curiosity

When do we stop asking questions? Anyone who has been around a bunch of five-year-olds knows they ask A LOT of questions. Research shows that small kids ask around 107 questions per hour.[1] As we grow up, this extraordinary number dwindles. Older children already ask fewer questions than their younger peers and by the time we reach adulthood, our curiosity falls off a cliff. At its core, curiosity is asking questions and asking questions is learning. As kids, we learn about the world around us by asking. Every answer we get shrinks our knowledge gap so by the time we reach adulthood, we know

---

[1] W.Berliner, Schools are killing curiosity: why we need to stop telling children to shut up and learn, *The Guardian* (January 2020). Available from: www.theguardian.com/education/2020/jan/28/schools-killing-curiosity-learn

enough to navigate the world and we stop asking (as many) questions. Curiosity and market research go hand in hand. American author and anthropologist, Zora Neale Hurston describes research as 'formalized curiosity. Poking and prying with purpose.'[2] Running a business is inviting your inner five-year-old back to stay. We're born curious and it's how we learn. We *can* be curious again. Diana Kander is a *New York Times* bestselling author, keynote speaker and curiosity expert. 'When it comes to understanding customers, curiosity is simply the gap between what you know and what you don't know,' Diana told me. Sounds obvious when you think about it, but the truth is very few of us wallow long enough in that space.

If I put you on the spot, you might not be able to articulate off the cuff your customer knowledge gaps. But I guarantee questions naturally pop into your head on a regular basis (that's curiosity right there!). *Why aren't my customers buying this? What format do my customers prefer when it comes to courses? Will customers still buy if I put my postage prices up? What do my customers find most useful?*

Top tip: Capture all those questions that seem to almost serendipitously pop into your mind over the course of your day: create a Question Bank. This can be a folder or document on your computer or a note on your phone. Every time a question arises, deposit it in your Question Bank. In no time you'll have identified that space, those gaps Diana referred to. The Question Bank is your starting point for taking curious action.

Born curious

Curiosity comes naturally to some of us. However, not every upbringing or work culture creates safe spaces for curiosity. On

---

[2] Z. Neale Hurston, *Dust Tracks on a Road*, Harper Perennial, p. 143 (1996).

the contrary, in some instances, asking why is risky and curiosity not always rewarded. Some of us may have been shut down at home, in the classroom or at work for asking too many questions. After all, *curiosity killed the cat*. If you were never really inspired to be curious, modelled curiosity or given the space to ask why, it might be more difficult to muster it up naturally.

But when it comes to customers, try we must.

If you are struggling to tap into your innate curiosity (I promise it's there somewhere), Anne-Laure Le Cunff has some brilliant advice on how we can foster more curiosity in our lives. Anne-Laure is the founder of Ness Labs, a writer and a neuroscience PhD researcher at King's College London. She agreed for me to share a few of her suggestions. Take note.

- **Ask questions**. Randomly ask yourself *Why?* and *How?* when reading something or chatting with a friend.
- **Read outside of your field**. Pick a type of book you would never naturally buy in a bookstore. Is it classic poetry? Non-fiction? A cookbook? Something about geology? Read it just for the sake of reading it.
- **Be inquisitive with people**. Choose someone in your entourage that you haven't seen in a while and invite them for coffee. Make it your goal to learn as much as possible about their interests. Take that approach any time you meet a new person.
- **Practise saying less**. Try to talk less and to listen more.
- **Hang out with a child**. Playing and talking with a child is probably one of the best reminders of our potential for curiosity.[3]

Curiosity is the explorer's prize tool. Identifying knowledge gaps then asking questions to fill them is how we'll learn about

---

[3] A-L. Le Cunff, *The science of curiosity: why we keep asking 'why'*, nesslabs.com. Available from: https://nesslabs.com/science-of-curiosity

customers. Practise curiosity at home and out in the wild. Make time for it. It will trickle back into your business behaviours soon enough. As an adult being curious is a choice. Make it.

Empathy

Next up in our explorer's toolkit is empathy. Empathy is having a moment. While it's always been at the heart of research practices, the COVID-19 pandemic really brought empathy into the public arena. LinkedIn is full of posts about being a more empathetic leader, employee or manager. CEOs are falling over themselves to show their empathetic nature and MBAs now include course material on empathy. Leaders are finally cottoning on to the fact that seeing and accepting people for who they wholly are; that listening and trying to understand people who are not like them makes for better working cultures. *Who knew?!*

Emotion researchers generally define empathy as the ability to sense other people's emotions, coupled with the ability to imagine what someone else might be thinking or feeling.[4] It's a few levels up from pity (I'm sorry for you) and sympathy (I feel for you) on the empathy spectrum. Empathy is the 'I feel with you'. Why do we need it in our business? When it comes to understanding customers, empathy helps you see the world from someone else's perspective. Empathy helps you take a walk in someone else's shoes. Empathy accepts the multitude of lived experiences beyond your own, without judgement, and it disarms bias. Empathy is not trying to convince (that you are right, and they are wrong) and it's not trying to change or advise. It's meeting customers where they are. Radical listening at its best.

---

[4] Greater Good Magazine, *Empathy defined*, Greater Good Magazine. Available from: https://greatergood.berkeley.edu/topic/empathy/definition

How to sharpen your empathy tool

Whether empathy is something we are genetically predisposed to or an innate trait we can nurture (researchers are still thrashing that one out[5]), you'll need a degree of empathy to run your small business effectively. If empathy it not your strong suit, if empathy rallies your woo radar, do your business a favour and rebrand it as a tool. An essential tool to figure out more effectively what your customers are feeling and thinking and why.

Adam Forbes is an entrepreneur and Program Director at Startupbootcamp. He suggests to his clients struggling to muster up customer empathy creating what marketers and researchers call *customer personas*.[6] A customer persona (avatar or profile) is a fictional representation of a customer. It's essentially a template with different sections you fill in with information about your customer. Sections range from the basic demographics (e.g. age, sex, income and occupation, ethnicity and religion) to hobbies, key challenges and aspirations. While the demographic stuff can be useful, it's always less revealing and insightful than customer psychographics, aspirations and behaviours.

Adam told me:

> For some people empathy comes very naturally and for other people, not so much. Creating customer personas has two benefits. The act of coming up with a persona forces you to step into someone else's shoes

---

[5] P. Streep, *6 things you need to know about empathy*, Psychology Today (January 2017). Available from: www.psychologytoday.com/gb/blog/tech-support/201701/6-things-you-need-know-about-empathy and Alex Therrien, *Genes have a role in empathy, study says* on BBC (March 2018). Available from: www.bbc.co.uk/news/health-43343807

[6] I guest edited this article www.couriermedia.com/article/creating-customer-personas/ for *Courier Magazine* if you fancy digging a little deeper into this topic.

(the empathy factor). That's the first benefit. And the second benefit is if there's more than one of you in your business, you can both do the exercise separately to help identify gaps and divergence in customer understanding.

All you need to get started is a pen and paper – you don't even need to have done any customer research. Personas are widespread practice in large businesses. For your business, they may well be surplus to requirements. But if you like a bit of structure and are keen to up your empathy game, they're a good place to start. You can find persona templates with a basic online search. Just remember, don't get too precious about them. They don't have to be perfectly designed and they will change as you learn more.

People watching is another wonderful way of building empathy with your audience. Do you run an in-person business? Brilliant. Observe your customers (subtly) and notice what they are doing. Are they rushing? Are they alone? Are they distracted? Are they checking their phone to see if they can buy a similar product on Amazon cheaper? Are they struggling around the shop floor with a wet umbrella?

A less structured but equally valuable method of sharpening your empathy tool is watching TV. I know! Permission to veg in front of Netflix. How often do you swap out the latest hit TV drama for a documentary? Documentaries and docuseries are windows into real lives we don't live. As with books, the right TV can help build empathy and strengthen our understanding of people who are not like us. Try it one night.

Ultimately empathy is a precursor for *why*. It helps us move from *I feel with my customer* (because I've spent time understanding them) to *I wonder why they feel that way?* and *I wonder why they do it that way?*

Courage

Courage is our third and final tool. Why are we talking about courage? If fear is stopping us doing the work, and if ego is fear in disguise, then courage is our much-needed antidote. Courage is often elevated to superhuman feats and exceptional actions. The courage we need in business is quieter, out of the spotlight but equally powerful. In a knowledge-is-power culture, it takes courage to admit we don't have all the answers. It takes courage to put our ideas out into the world with no guarantees of what we'll get back. When done right, market research is exposing. We test assumptions that we hold tight. We share our ideas with real people, and we get feedback we might not want to hear (see Chapter 10 for how to take feedback like a champ). Market research is a vulnerable sport. You might not feel very brave right now, but courage in business, like curiosity and empathy, is something you can practise.

We can't be curious, empathetic and brave all the time. But we can aspire to use these tools more of the time, especially when it comes to customers. We'll all have different definitions of what that looks like depending on our starting point. For some, brave might be reaching out to a friendly customer for the first time to ask for 30 minutes of their time, for others it will mean pitching for investment after a successful product launch. Find your flavour of brave and run with it.

To sum up

This chapter has given you three tools to run better businesses: curiosity, empathy and courage. Far from being nebulous concepts, these three tools are ones you'll reach for time and time again on your quest to understand customers better. Some of you might already feel well equipped (tools sharp and ready to go). On the other hand, some of you might have realized that you'll need a bit more time to sharpen yours. And that's fine too.

With our foundations firmly in place, we're now going to move on to the practical stuff. While the first three chapters of this book have purposely dwelled on the *why* we need market research, the *what's* holding us back and *what* tools do we need to build our explorer's toolkit, in the following chapters, we'll start chipping away at the *how*. How to understand customers? How do we know what methods to use? How do we ask good questions? How do we know if we're on the right track? In Chapter 4, we'll start with the most underused but business-changing market research method out there: customer interviews.

Chapter 3 recap:

- When it comes to your customers, adopt a beginners' mindset (even if you've been beavering away on your business for years).

- Channel your inner five-year-old and ask more questions.

- Create your own Question Bank for capturing questions about your customers.

- Curiosity never *actually* killed the cat.

- Empathy is having a moment, get on board.

- Courage is the antidote to fear.

- Curiosity, empathy and courage are essential business tools you can sharpen.

4 I met Alcatraz prisoner 1259, talking to customers and how to just ask

William Baker spent three months in Alcatraz jail. The Rock. His number was 1259. I spotted him in the prison, near the gift shop. He was signing his book and lapping up the kind of attention an actual ex-Alcatraz prisoner would.

On the ferry back to San Francisco pier, I spotted him again. Let's ask for a photo, I said to my son. What a story to bring back to Blighty.

So, we asked, and William happily obliged. You have to ask, you see. Hold your expectations lightly. But ask anyway (I didn't even buy his book).

Extract from Jungle Juice, 6th June 2022

I n this chapter you will learn about one of the most powerful ways of doing market research: interviewing customers. I'll share some of the different methods you can use and when to use them. You'll discover all the places you can find people to interview. Then I'll give some tips for those of you already breaking out in a sweat at the thought of asking someone for their time, so that you can ask with confidence.

What is a customer interview?

Speaking to people intentionally is the fastest way to learn about your customers. It's a game changer. And most of you aren't doing it. Not systematically to understand customers. Perhaps you didn't realize it was something you could do to improve your business? Maybe you don't have a clue where to start? What to ask? Or maybe you're mortified by the very idea of asking customers for their time and getting a no. Read on, you'll be fine.

In research lingo, interviewing people is a qualitative research method. What do we mean by that? It means the answers and insights you get are words, not numbers (like you would get with a survey). Customer interviews (also called user interviews) are the best way businesses can get customer insight straight from the horse's mouth. They reveal insights you can't get through any other research method. In simple terms, a customer interview is a conversation during which you ask customers a set of questions. Topics range from the use of your products or service, to customer behaviours, motivations and habits.

Talking to people is more time consuming up front than just getting on with creating your new offer. Sure. I call it front loading – putting in a bit more effort at the beginning to avoid things getting messy at the end. This saves time in the long run. The insights and evidence you'll get from speaking to customers will help you make decisions on all the other stuff that needs doing. Is it scary? For some of you, maybe. Is it uncomfortable? Sometimes. But the benefit it brings is worth the fleeting feelings of discomfort.

There are different ways to interview people. I have highlighted the most common ones in Table 1 with their respective pros and cons.

Table 1: Interviewing methods

Method	Pros	Cons
Face-to-face aka in-real-life (IRL)	IRL human connection, body language and tone	Time consuming, privacy, space
Remote face-to-face (Zoom, etc.)	Quick to set up, can have more than one in a day, convenient for participant	Technology failure, less personable
Telephone	No video (some people prefer)	Harder to record, hard to read body language
Email	Less intimidating, less energy	Not able to ask follow-up questions, nuances and spontaneousness of responses lost. Risk of self-censoring is greater
Focus groups	Interact with multiple people in one session	Group think and bias. I would not recommend unless you are a highly skilled and experienced facilitator

It's worth expanding briefly on the cons of focus groups presented in Table 1. A focus group is when you bring together a group of people to ask them a series of questions. Focus groups are usually a false economy. It may feel like you're killing two birds (or three or four) with one stone but unless you are a skilled facilitator (as in pro), the insights you get are unlikely to be a true reflection of what each individual contributor really thinks and feels about the topic in question. You've been warned, proceed with caution.

When to use customer interviews?

Interviewing customers can answer pretty much every *why* and *how* question you have. *Why did you buy this? Why didn't you buy that? How did you go about choosing that product? Tell me about the last time you looked for a candle online. Talk me through the last time you booked a holiday.*

There is little a customer interview cannot bring you. Broadly speaking there are three types of customer interviews you need to know about:

1. Exploratory (or generative)
2. Contextual
3. Continuous

Most of your conversations with customers will be exploratory but as you get a little more experienced you might want to try the other two types (contextual and continuous). Let's take a look.

Exploratory (or generative) interviews help you understand first-hand who your customers are (as humans, *not* as users) and their everyday lived experiences. Folks over at User Interviews, a user research recruitment platform, describe exploratory conversations as 'a style of interviewing that allows us to dig into a person's identity beyond their screen, and beyond their interaction with [a] product.'[1]

This is where I recommend you spend most of your time. Use exploratory interviews to dive into customer behaviours, habits, opinions and motivations. You can also use them for idea generation. They're great when you have a hunch about an unmet need or just want to explore and identify new opportunities. The User Interviews team adds:

---

[1] User Interviews, *The UX Research Field Guide*, userinterviews.com. Available from: www.userinterviews.com/ux-research-field-guide-chapter/user-interviews

User interviews *really* shine during discovery, when you still don't really know exactly the problem you're trying to solve or how. You might have a general idea about what a problem is, in which case generative interviews can help you refine your understanding. Or you may simply want to develop a product in a given space, and you need to generate ideas about what problems exist before you can imagine their solutions.[2]

Contextual interviews allow you to observe and interview your customer in their own environment. You watch them *doing* the thing (booking a holiday, navigating your website, buying clothes, writing content, etc.) and you ask them questions while they complete tasks. Contextual interviews can be used for testing products and services. This is more commonly referred to as usability testing.

Contextual interviews feel more involved in our increasingly virtual culture but as UX researcher and designer Trina Moore Pervall told me, being creative can go a long way:

> I was working for a client on a mobile app for voice-enabling recipes. Not that many people are going to invite you into their house to sit and watch how they cook. So, I asked a few people in my network if they would agree for me to observe them remotely, using Zoom. I was able to follow what they were doing and ask questions at the same time. It wasn't as good as an in-person experience, but it was good enough to get the insights I needed.

---

[2] User Interviews, *The UX Research Field Guide*, userinterviews.com. Available from: www.userinterviews.com/ux-research-field-guide-chapter/user-interviews

Depending on your business, being creative could mean asking someone in your co-working space if you could watch them complete a specific online task (for example, trying to find the testimonial section on your website, buying a gift for their kids or doing the weekly online shop). Remember if you're not able to look over someone's shoulder in real life, digital proxies can work too. A proxy is another term for the next best thing. In Trina's case, she couldn't physically be in the same room as the person she was interviewing so she used Zoom (a proxy) instead.

Finally, continuous interviews (or what I like to call pulse conversations) involve speaking to customers little and often. The term was coined by Teresa Torres. In an interview with Awkward Silences, Teresa explained: 'The value of continuous interviewing is really just being reminded on a regular basis that our customers will always know their world better than we possibly could.'[3] Continuous interviewing involves speaking to customers as a regular practice, not just when you are working towards finding something out. Teresa recommends weekly for businesses with the right resources in place. For smaller businesses, this may feel onerous but continuous interviewing can take on a number of more manageable forms such as making a point of striking up a conversation with customers in your shop or café (if you run a bricks and mortar business) or lingering a bit longer on social media to strike up some digital conversations. Whether you opt for exploratory, contextual or continuous discovery interviews, you won't get very far if you've nobody to speak to.

---

[3] Awkward Silences podcast by User Interviews, Episode 23, August 2019. Teresa Torres interviewed by Erin May. https://www.userinterviews.com/blog/how-to-interview-customers-continuously-with-teresa-torres-of-product-talk

Where to find people?

Where do I find people to speak to? Valid question. One I get asked ALL the time. I usually respond with another question: How many people do you know?

Me? A musician. A DJ. An actor. A broadsheet journalist. A GP. A semi-pro goalkeeper. A headteacher. A nurse. A dog trainer. A kidney surgeon. A TV presenter. A supermarket checkout agent. A cleaner. A social worker. A Spanish diplomat (who narrowly escaped Ukraine). A university lecturer. A campaigner. A falafel maker in my local mall. A CEO. An award-winning broadcaster. A French dog groomer. A village mayor. A nursery worker. A job seeker. A tax-avoider. A 200k+ followers' influencer. At a push... Brian Ferry (story on request).

I could go on. My point? The average human knows 600 people. We are only ever six introductions away from someone else on this planet.[4] Fact. Now we could debate the definition of *know* but I bet you have people to speak to. You might just need a little help. Here are a few places to find customers (or target customers) to speak to.

1. Your customers

Doctor Susan Moore is a behavioural marketing consultant. Her motto: 'It's easier to push an open door.' So true. If you pluck random people off the street and ask them whether they'd be happy to spare 30 minutes for a customer interview, nine times out of ten you'll get a no. So, start where the door is already ajar. First stop, your existing customer community. If you have a business, then you have customers. At least some. Whether

---

[4] D. Smith, 'Poof! Just six degrees of separation between us' in *The Guardian* (August 2008). Available from: www.theguardian.com/technology/2008/aug/03/internet.email

they're paying you for a product or service or you're currently offering something for free, they are customers. So, draw on this group first (more on how to ask later in this chapter). A short email after a purchase, a follow-up email to a past client, a pop-up on your website, a request in your newsletter or on your social media. Ask. If you're in the process of building a business and don't have any paying customers yet, then start with your assumed target customers (the people you think you'll be targeting for your product or service). More ideas on how to find those later in this section.

2. Lapsed customers

Customers no more? They can still be useful. They've only bought once, never to return. Unsubscribed or decided your product or service is surplus to requirements. Doesn't mean they haven't got something to say. In fact, people with no skin in the game are great people to speak to. They don't hold back, have no relationship to jeopardize and tend to be more honest with their views (they might need a sweetener, we'll look at incentives a little later in this chapter). If you have an online shop, most analytics suites allow you to segment customers. You can identify those who have only bought once and the lurkers (the ones who come to the website over and over, signed up to your newsletter, but never buy).

3. Mailing list

If you have a mailing list – a list of emails collected over the years – then you have people to talk to. Your mailing list will be made up of people who are genuinely interested in whatever it is you sell or say. They make a great pool of peeps to pick from. Your email subscribers are often a warm and willing crowd, especially if you've been building up healthy relationships through frequent (ish) emailing. If you haven't started collecting emails yet or you're not writing to your subscribers on a regular basis, take this as encouragement to start.

4. Social media

Are you on social media? Instagram. Threads. Twitter. TikTok. LinkedIn. Facebook. Discord. If you have followers likely to be interested in your business, then you have people to speak to. You don't have to have a huge following on social media to find willing people. As with your mailing list, your social media following is generally built up of people interested in what you have to say or sell. Many of these platforms allow you to ask questions, create polls and more broadly generate engagement with your online communities. The simple question, *Can anyone spare 30 minutes to talk to me?*, is only a few clicks away.

5. Alumni

LinkedIn is a great one for this. Even if your business is not an obvious shot for LinkedIn, of all the peeps you have accumulated over a lifetime, chances are half of them have found their way to the biggest professional social networking platform. Reach out, build connections and if they are in your target market, ask away. If you don't know how to reach out to someone you haven't spoken to since you were smoking cheeky fags behind the bike shed, try this:

> Hi Ruth, congratulations on your new role [or whatever latest news they have posted]. Can you believe it's been nearly five years since we were at [insert school/company] together?! I currently run my own coaching business and am looking for some middle managers in the HR sector to talk through their current challenges. I'd love to set up some time to ask you a few questions.

Wherever you originally know them from, if you're stuck for how to approach them, use this six-point email template guide:

1. Greeting
2. Your hook (reference to something they have recently shared)
3. Reference to your shared past (previous job, university, etc.)
4. Your update [I run my own business doing X]
5. The ask [can I have 30 minutes of your time OR would you know anyone I could speak to]
6. Options [zoom or on the phone at these times]

Job done.

6. Personal network

Dog walker, cleaner, gym buddies, school gate parents, Saturday football club fans, choir pals, co-working colleagues. Tap into your real-world network. By network I mean all the people who float in and out of your life on a regular basis. You can find people to talk to for market research in the most unexpected places.

7. Friends of friends

For bias reasons, friends are a big no (see upcoming point nine on this list), but friends of friends? Go for it. I once found five men (five yesses) in a day for a client who needed to get her head around male gift-buying habits by tapping into my friends of friends network. These five friends were all willing to ask their male friends or partners on my behalf. I asked the partner of my bestie, an ex-colleague of my partner's, two dog-walking pals met during lockdown, and my own partner. They all said yes. By asking friends to ask their friends/partners, you increase your chances of getting a yes because someone else, who they know and trust, is doing the asking.

8. Third parties

If you have some budget, you can also outsource the whole recruiting process to a third party. This approach works well if your target audience is hard to reach or is in a different country (with unfamiliar cultures or languages to your own). When using a third party, always make sure you ask about the screening process as you want to be 100% sure they are recruiting people in your target market.

9. Friends and family

And finally, close friends and family. Seriously don't go there. Often, they will only tell you what you want to hear. They mean well so indulge them lightly (nice of them to feel involved especially if they're forking out any cash to support you) but don't take their word as gospel. Keep them for support. A safe place to vent but don't base your business strategy on what they think.

So please don't tell me you don't have anyone to reach out to. Want to do the brain dump now? Give the next stretch task a try. If your brain is already frazzled, come back to it when you're feeling fresh.

Stretch task #4

- Grab an A4 sheet of paper and a pen.
- Fold the paper in half and in half again. Hey presto, eight squares.
- Set your timer for 10 minutes.

- In each square, write the name of someone you could ask – how you know them (are they a customer, a neighbour in your target market, your mate from the gym?), how you'll contact them and when.
- Don't overthink it, just start writing.
- No pen and paper? No problem. Use your phone.

How to ask

How to ask should be on the school curriculum. You get places when you ask although asking is way harder for some than others. My mum taught me to ask by modelling it. Every. Damn. Day. It was excruciatingly embarrassing half the time. I had the mum who marched up to whatever authority was in question that day and requested an extension, an apology, an exception, an explanation. I hated it. Until I realized, she was right all along.

You don't need to be a full-on extrovert to ask. Asking quietly is just as effective. The most useful bit of wisdom I can impart on this matter is to ask as if your life depends on it. Thankfully, for most of us, it doesn't. But channelling that spirit can move mountains. I've done it many times. As a news reporter in crowed spaces, as a lost tourist in faraway lands and as a mother of a child who needs a pee… NOW. These days we can ask without picking up the phone (email, direct messages, WhatsApp, etc.). And for a lot of us, that's a good thing (phone phobia is real).

When we ask, we might get a no. We might also get a yes. Often, in fact. Most people *will* say yes if you ask for their time. Especially when you're a small business. People like small. They can relate to small (actual human beings on the other end). Once you get them talking, you'll realize that most people also like talking about themselves. And that's essentially what you want them to do. How to ask might be obvious to some. For those who can already feel the panic rising in their chest, I have a framework to calm your nerves. Follow my C.A.N. (do) method:

- **Context**. First explain why you're asking. Educate your audience that it's good practice to ask for their input. This will set you up for future success. Tell them you're not asking them to buy something (this is NOT a sales call) and that you just want to understand how they go about (insert as appropriate e.g. doing their marketing, buying presents, relaxing, treating themselves, their finances, etc.).
- **Ask**. State the ask. You really care about your customers, and you'd like some of their time to understand them better. Be specific with how much time you need. I'd suggest a minimum of 30 minutes and a maximum of 60 minutes (the sweet spot is probably about 45 minutes). If you plan to provide an incentive, this is the moment to tell them.
- **Nitty gritty**. Give as many details as you can upfront. Where do you want it to take place? Do you have a preference? Or present them with options. Being as specific as possible shows respect for the other person's time. Aim to get a yes in as few interactions as possible. 'I have availability Tuesday and Thursday between 9.30am–12pm' is better than a vague 'I could do anytime next week'. That way your customer has all the information at hand to decide quickly. You could get a date in the diary in one email exchange. Alternatively, use one of those online calendars like Calendly and get people to select themselves.

Still feeling a little stuck? Here's a sample email script I use. Amend as necessary.

Hi Angel, it's Katie here from Product Jungle®. One of my priorities this year is to review some of the ways I deliver my services. I really want to make sure I'm making the right decisions by my customers. I would appreciate it if you could spare 30 minutes or so to talk to me about how you currently go about [insert as appropriate].

To show my appreciation for your time, I would offer you a £10 gift card.

I have availability Wednesday and Thursday next week between 9.30am–2pm. Alternatively, you can book directly using this link [insert link to appropriate booking tool].

Thanks so much, I look forward to hearing back from you,

Katie

If you intend to record the conversation (it's so much easier if you do), you'll need to ask your customer for consent before you speak to them. Most people will agree (if the recording is strictly used for research purposes and won't be shared) but if they don't, it's time to get nifty with the notetaking. There are a few other rules and best practices to adhere to when handling customer conversations, recordings and transcripts. Be sure to check them out in Chapter 13 of this book.

While we're on the topic of recording, once you get consent, stick a PRESS RECORD reminder on the top of your computer (talking from experience). If you happen to be interviewing someone on their account (as opposed to yours) plan accordingly, as you might not have the permissions to press record (also speaking from experience!).

In summary, reframe asking customers for their time as a duty of care. You're doing it so you can create stuff they'll love, find useful and want to buy. And do you know what? Almost every customer interview I've done has been enjoyable for both parties. Some have even found it cathartic (their words not mine). As I said, people love to talk about themselves.

Incentives

Incentives work. Real incentives work even better. Being part of a prize draw for a huge audience will not carry that much gravitas (odds of winning are so low). With smaller audiences, it carries a little more weight. Think creatively and be willing to set aside a small budget to properly reward people for their time (some suggestions on amounts in Chapter 13). That said, I have secured many interviews for businesses without incentives. If you're tight on cash, it's possible. Research best practice suggests you avoid rewarding customers with your own branded products or services in exchange for their time to avoid conflicts of interest. However, there are other ways to sweeten the deal, here are a few ideas:

- Prize draw
- Cash
- Donation to a charity of their choice (have a pre-selected list of charities)
- Gift card or voucher

Getting over yourself

Some of you will still struggle to ask, despite all the advice in this chapter. Here are a few recurring rebuttals I come across with clients and a few ways you can overcome them. They might come in handy when your mind starts playing tricks.

- **What if I'm wrong?** True. What if you share your idea and nobody bites? What if you realize that you were wrong about your audience? That's learning right there. Embrace it. Better to know early and tweak accordingly than crash and burn later. Just saying.

- **What if they say no?** Will people think I'm opportunistic? Probably not. Will they think I'm trying to sell them something? Maybe (tell them you're not). Will they say no? Also, maybe. Will that feel uncomfortable? Briefly. If you're scared of a no, start with a friendly customer.
- **What if it's too late?** We're back to the sunk cost fallacy (Chapter 1). I get it, it's hard turning back when you're already so far down the road. Think of it more as a detour. Remember, it's never too late to get close and personal with the people you serve.

There's no magic solution to moving through these natural feelings of discomfort. But with practice, and the tips I've given you in this chapter, you CAN get comfortable with the uncomfortable feeling of asking someone for something. Jane Frost CBE and CEO of the MRS told me: 'Market research, it's not rocket science. It's respect.' Let's channel that.

Creating a discussion guide

Talking of respect, the amount of preparation you put into your interview is a form of respect. It lets your interviewee know that this conversation is important. That customers matter. Once you have some customers willing to talk, it's time to prepare. For a 30-minute conversation draft 3–5 questions, if you manage to secure 60 minutes, double that. I always draft a few extra questions just in case the person I'm speaking to is quite concise and we get through the planned questions with time to spare. Remember, you don't need to ask ALL the things. Focus your conversations (and questions) on a couple of key learning opportunities each time. When

I say prepare the interview, I don't mean script the whole conversation word for word. But drawing up a discussion guide has huge benefits. A discussion guide:

- Makes sure you have all the important topics and questions covered (because it forces you to think about it beforehand).
- Keeps the conversation on track. It's easy for you or your customer to go off topic or to lose your train of thought. (Use phrases like 'I just wanted to come back to… ', 'So sorry to interrupt but I want to come back to something you said earlier' or 'Oh dear we are going off topic, my fault, let's get back to my last questions' to get chats back on track.)
- Makes the sensemaking part easier (when you need to review and compare multiple interview notes, see Chapter 6 for how to do that).
- Reminds you to ask for some of the basic demographic information either at the start or at the end of the interview.

The questions you draft for your discussion guide will depend on what you're trying to find out. If you are working through this book and at this point want to jot down some questions, please do. You might already have deposited some in your newly created Question Bank I referred to in Chapter 3. Keep those questions warm and revisit them when you get to the next chapter. In customer research, there is such a thing as a stupid question, as you'll soon find out.

Next, a few tips on the interview itself.

During the interview

Shut up! is what I write on a sticky note before I interview a customer. I stick it somewhere visible (to me). I lean towards the extrovert side of the spectrum when it comes to human interactions. I ask lots of questions, I'm hyper curious and prone to talking too much. I get easily carried away with the conversation and can't wait to ask the next question. If I am not careful, I find myself butting in before the person has finished answering the previous question. Whether you identify more as an extrovert or introvert, keep your discussion guide with you during the interview (a printout of it works well). It sounds obvious but it's easy to get flustered if you only have one screen. A discussion guide is not only practical from a memory and interview structure point of view, but it also helps offset any natural conversational preferences. More specifically, it:

- Avoids you talking too much
- Keeps your mind focused (if you're feeling a little nervous)
- Helps you feel prepared (you are)

Research authority NN/g has a comprehensive list of things on their website to take into consideration when conducting an interview.[5] I have summarized some of the most relevant ones for you here:

1. Show your customer you are **listening** by making eye contact, nodding and offering *I am listening to you* cues such as 'I see'.
2. **Don't interrupt** them, however keen you are to ask the next questions. If you do, apologize, and allow them to continue.
3. **Don't rush** or speak too fast. Pause. Embrace the awkward silences. Its uncomfortable but you get used to it.

---

[5] K. Pernice, *User interviews: how, when, and why to conduct them*, Nielsen Norman Group (NN/g) (October 2018). Available from: www.nngroup.com/articles/user-interviews

People need time to think. Give them that time. Some of the best insights emerge after a silence.

4. **Slow down** your pace of speech. Talking slowly has a calming effect and indicates that you are not anxious and that you have time to listen.

5. Start with some **warm-up questions** that are easy to answer. But beware of questions that could lead to your interlocuter feeling judged in anyway. NN/g gives a great example. Instead of *What was the last book you read?* try *What do you like to do in your spare time?*

6. Be as **authentic** as possible and as NN/g says: 'Don't fake empathy... It is better to be yourself; don't say something if you don't genuinely feel it.'[6]

After the interview

Congratulations. You have your first interview under your belt (or will do soon). A few housekeeping tips for after the interview:

- Check the interview was recorded and saved somewhere you'll find it.
- Use a transcribe tool if you can, to get a transcript of your conversation (I recommend the tool Grain but there are plenty of other options out there).
- Read through any manual notes you took and use highlighter to illuminate anything that grabbed your attention or piqued your curiosity (10–15 minutes max).
- Send a follow-up email thanking the person for their time and asking whether they'd be happy for you to contact them with any follow-up questions if necessary.

---

[6] K. Pernice, *User interviews: how, when, and why to conduct them,* Nielsen Norman Group (NN/g) (October 2018). Available from: www.nngroup.com/articles/user-interviews

To sum up

If you only take one thing away from this book, let it be this. SPEAK TO REAL PEOPLE. Talk to your customers. Have conversations. Set up interviews. Don't spend all your time hiding behind surveys, focus groups and feedback forms. Nothing beats it. It'll do wonders for your confidence and sharpen your decision making, and it'll give you a leg up over the competition. Guaranteed.

I've told you why talking to people is so important. I've showed you where to find people to speak to and the benefits of preparing (versus the I'll-figure-it-out-as-I-go-along style of interviewing). Time to craft some actual questions. In the next chapter, we'll make sure they're the right ones. Folks, believe me when I say there is such a thing as a stupid question.

Chapter 4 recap:

- Customer interviews are one of the best ways to understand your people.

- You can and will find people to speak to (you know more people than you think).

- Use the C.A.N. method (Context, Ask, Nitty Gritty) to get over any awkward emotions and ask.

- Sweeten the deal with incentives where appropriate.

- Create a discussion guide to keep conversations on track.

- Customer interviews are about listening more than you talk.

- Remember to press Record!

5 The mother of all theories and there is such a thing as a stupid question

When was the last time you lied to a business? Me? A few times. Not to a business per se. But a charity in the business of rescuing dogs. I promised Trish she could call me back. That yes, I was considering sponsoring Molly, the doe-eyed mongrel. That yes, the cute sponsor pack they'd pop in the post would make a nice Christmas gift for the kids. I LIED. I didn't want to hurt Trish's feelings. For her to think I didn't care about dogs (I do). For weeks, the unidentified number flashed up on my phone. Trish gave up.

Stop asking customers whether they're interested in your product or service. Stop asking customers whether they'd buy what you're selling. Not outright. Cold. Customers lie, especially when they have nothing to lose. No skin in the game. Half-truths buzzing around like flies near a dog turd.

Extract from Jungle Juice, 6th March 2022

Not all questions you ask customers are created equal. And there is such a thing as a stupid question when it comes to understanding customers. Questions that will lead you down the wrong path. This chapter is important. I'll give you my five golden rules for asking great questions. Stick to them and they'll change your business.

First, let's get properly acquainted with JTBD theory. I gave JTBD a namecheck back in Chapter 2. If you remember, I explained customers don't always know what they want but they nearly always know what they're trying to get done. JTBD helps us do just that. Let's start with an example.

Jobs to be done (JTBD) theory

In the late 1990s, McDonald's got it wrong. Big time! The fast-food giant wanted to boost milkshake sales. It profiled and surveyed its milkshake punters. *More flavours?* it asked. *Why not?* customers said. McDonald's introduced more flavours but sales flatlined.

So, they called in the late Harvard Professor, Clayton Christensen. His team spent two days watching and talking (think asking questions) to McDonald's shake shoppers. His findings? Customers bought milkshakes to do very specific *jobs*: offset a boring drive to work; keep their mouths and (one) hand busy and keep their bellies full for longer.

Armed with this new insight, McDonald's made some changes. It introduced thicker milkshakes (these took longer to drink, and customers stayed full for longer) and a faster and more convenient checkout process (which suited busy commuters trying to get to work on time). Shake sales increased sevenfold.

Clayton used the JTBD framework to understand what McDonald's customers were *hiring* the milkshake for. He asked the right questions and got insight that boosted the fast-food giant's bottom line.

So, what exactly is JTBD and how can you apply it to your business? JTBD is a lens through which we understand people. Over the years, it revolutionized the way many successful businesses go about understanding their customers but rarely finds its way to smaller businesses. The BIG idea is that customers go about their days getting (or trying to get) stuff done. In their work and in their life. We call the stuff they're trying to get done *jobs*. A job can be deciding what shampoo to use, which car to buy or what to do with your kids on a wet weekend. A job can be to relax, fix the toilet seat, level up in French, find healthy food options on the go, make a boring commute more enjoyable or sort out your relationship. The American business strategist Anthony Ulwick is credited with first shaping the concept back in the 1990s. He has written (and still does) extensively on the topic. However, more recently, JTBD is associated with the works and teachings (and milkshake musings) of Clayton Christensen.

This approach is ground-breaking because it reframes our products and services as things customers hire (think buy and use) to get *jobs* done. Once we figure out what jobs they're trying to get done by hiring a product or service (maybe ours, maybe someone else's), we can work out how to help them get that job done better, faster and more rewardingly. This isn't some business theory only relevant to the tech world or B2B (business-to-business), this idea works for candles, watches, course creators, cars and, as we'll find out later in this chapter, even toilet roll.

JTBD changes the way businesses ask questions from *What do you want?* to *What are you trying to get done?* Ultimately jobs tend to last, while products don't. And over time, one job (listening to music for example) will be satisfied with a myriad of solutions and products (gramophone, cassette player, turntable, CD, smart phones, Alexa…). Jobs theory allows you to innovate on the how without being tied to one single solution.

JTBD also helps us view our products and services beyond their functional use and encourages us to think about the other stuff that goes on (social and emotional factors) when making a purchase decision. Finally, JTBD shakes up how we view our competitors.

What are your customers trying to get done?

Think about it. How can you apply this thinking to your business? What is your customer *hiring* your product or service for? What *job* are they ultimately trying get done? If you can figure that out, you can help them get it done better, quicker and easier. So, whether you're selling milkshakes, t-shirts or online courses, don't assume people just want more flavours.

Beyond the functional

One of the most useful aspects of the JTBD theory is how it helps businesses embrace the social and emotional aspects of what drives consumer behaviour. This is important these days, as there are hundreds if not thousands of businesses offering essentially the same product. If everyone was choosing products based on their functional uses, there wouldn't be any need for so much choice. However, customers are humans, so emotions are always involved.

JTBD break *jobs* into three main categories: functional jobs, emotional jobs and social jobs. *Functional* jobs are the easiest to grasp and the category we feel most comfortable exploring as small businesses (e.g. I buy a car to get from A to B). *Social* is all about how things make your customer look (in society) as a result of choosing a certain product to get a *job* done (e.g. I buy a Tesla car for social kudos), while *emotional* is about how the purchase makes your customer feel (e.g. I feel good buying a Tesla because it's electric and I care about the environment).

Emotional and social jobs can be ripe with opportunity for businesses because they are so often overlooked by our competitors. Co-authors Stephen Wunker, Jessica Wattman and David Farber in their book *Jobs to Be Done*, observed the following:

Emotional jobs tend to be neglected in business especially outside the realm of consumer package goods such as food and cleaning products... as competitors find ways to satisfy the same functional jobs at a lower price point, emotional elements can provide a vital way to differentiate your product.[1]

Table 2: Examples of functional, emotional and social jobs

Product/ Service	Functional job	Social job	Emotional job
Rolex watch	Telling the time	Show you can afford it, convey status and success	Reward yourself, have an heirloom to pass down, investment piece
Who Gives a Crap toilet paper	Wiping your backside	Look how cool I am, look how much I care about the environment	I am a good person, I choose brands that care and that makes me feel good
Monopoly	Playing board game	We are a family that plays board games instead of being glued to our screens	Family bonding time makes me feel like a better parent

---

[1] S. Wunker, J. Wattman and D. Farber, *Jobs to Be Done: A Roadmap for Customer-Centered Innovation*, AMACOM, pp. 31–32 (2017).

PhD at 50 years old	Qualifying as a doctor	Status and respect that comes with the title Doctor	Prove to yourself that it's never too late, self-acceptance
Co-working space	Space to work away from home	Shows others you have a serious business, portrays the entrepreneur life	Combat loneliness, make friends, create healthy work/ life boundaries

Do you see? Nobody buys a Rolex watch to tell the time. You buy a Rolex watch to show status (social). To show you can afford it (social). To treat yourself (emotional). To pass down an heirloom (emotional and social) once you've popped your clogs and to fit in with the rest of the Rolex-wearing crowd. If you just wanted to tell the time, you'd have bought a £5 watch on Amazon.

My favourite toilet roll brand is Who Gives a Crap. This is clearly a business that has gone beyond exploring the functional use of its product (wiping your backside) when it comes to its customers. What this brand understands about its customers is then ploughed back into its positioning and marketing and no doubt its innovation. Let's take a look.

Who Gives a Crap is the coolest toilet paper brand on the planet. The toilet roll industry was ripe for innovation. Who knew? This business understands me and how toilet paper fits into my life. They've tapped deep into the things I care about (beyond the obvious). Customer understanding at its best:

- The toilet paper is sustainable. Made of bamboo (grows back seven times faster than trees). I care about the planet.

- The company gives 50% of its profits to charities that ensure everyone has access to clean water and a toilet. This makes me feel good spending a little more.
- It has parents in mind with crazy big box (loo rolls delivered in boxes of 48) craft ideas. Kid does crafts = good parent vibes + 10 minutes peace.
- It partners with artists for special edition wrapping. How cool! I love cool (I think I'm cool).
- At Christmas, the brand encourages you to use the festive edition wrap to package presents (even includes handy *To… From…* labels). A Christmas conversation starter AND giving me all the good green vibes.
- The last eight rolls or so of the box are wrapped in red paper with a warning message saying you're about to run out. I have a busy life. The red nudge helps me and avoids the 'who used the last loo roll?' argument. A winner all round.

Could I buy cheaper toilet rolls? Sure. But Who Gives a Crap doesn't worry about that. I'm their ideal customer and they know it. Whatever your product or your service, explore beyond the functional. Lean deep into YOUR customers with JTBD in mind. You'll be onto something. I promise.

Competitors

One last thing about JTBD before we get to what questions to ask customers. Until now you might believe your competitors are other businesses selling the same stuff as you. JTBD blows that theory out of the water and frames competitors as other products or services that help customers get the same job done. Let's revisit our watch example.

A Rolex watch competitor could be a Louis Vuitton suitcase or a membership to an exclusive members' club in Mayfair,

London – both of these fulfil some of the same social and emotional jobs our customer is after.

Five golden rules for asking quality questions

Keeping JTBD in mind, let's dive into the type of questions you should ask your customers because all the answers you need so often reside with them. Here are my five golden rules for asking questions. While the goal is to use these questions (and avoid others) in customer interviews, keep them in your back pocket for when you have ad hoc encounters with your audience. In your shop, in the lift, at an event or at your local market. One good question can change everything.

1. Ask open-ended questions

Closed questions won't get you far. Open is what we're after. Closed questions are ones that are typically answered by yes or no. *Do you enjoy outdoor swimming?* Yes. *Do you file your tax return at the last minute?* Yes. *Do penguins eat peaches?* Umm... pass. Closed questions are brilliant for customer surveys (I'll show you why in Chapter 7). But when you are having a real-life conversation with a customer, whether face-to-face or online, avoid them. Closed questions cut things short, and they prevent you from getting to the good stuff. Open-ended questions, as the name implies, throw customer conversations wide open. *Tell me about the last time you went swimming outside. What else do you do to relax? Talk me through how it feels to do your tax return. To what extent do penguins eat peaches?* Can you see the shift? Open-ended questions unlock customer stories that allow you to experience the world through your customers' eyes. They build rapport and trust (customers feel listened to). It helps businesses empathize and understand context (behaviours, motivations, habits and quirks). Stories teach you everything.

Let's take a fictional example with a micro-business we will call Bright run by accountant Mohamed. Bright offers accounting services to SMEs, typically 20+ employees. Mohamed is considering expanding his offer and launching a tax return service for the self-employed. He isn't sure whether there will be enough demand for it to be worth it, so he sets up some interviews with a couple of self-employed people from his network.

Here are two fictionalized conversations. The first using closed questions and the second using open-ended questions. Spot the difference.

Conversation 1 (**closed** questions):

M: How often do you do your accounting for tax purposes?
Interviewee: Once a quarter.

M: Do you enjoy doing it?
Interviewee: No, I hate it.

M: Do you use Excel to track your expenses?
M: I should do but I don't, no.

Conversation 2 (**open-ended** questions):

M: Tell me about the last time you did your accounts.
Interviewee: I aim to do them once a quarter, but it rarely works out that way. I probably have a quick look a few months before my tax return is due. I really do need to get a better system in place.

M: Talk me through how you went about filing your tax return last year.
Interviewee: It was a nightmare, I got so stressed. I started out with good intentions and aimed to fill it in and pay a month before the deadline. I never pay early as someone once recommended that I put my tax money in a high interest account until the payment

deadline. Although to be honest, I never got around to doing it. Anyway, I ended up filing my return the day before the deadline and I swear I forgot some of the expenses.

M: How do you normally go about keeping track of your expenses?
Interviewee: When it's online, I try to remember to send myself a copy of the invoice for any business purchases. I have an expense folder in my inbox and try to take pictures of receipts although they are not in a dedicated folder on my phone, so it always takes me ages to find them.

Do you see how a simple shift of questioning gets richer insights?

A good question is like a nutcracker. It prises the conversation wide open. Here are some of the most effective open-ended question starters:

- Tell me about…
- To what extent…
- How do you currently go about…
- Walk me through…
- Talk me through…

Check out my own Question Bank at the end of this book for more open-ended question ideas. Remember, think open, think stories, their stories. You shut up (mostly), listen and learn.

2. Avoid leading questions

Asking leading questions is another easy mistake to make when we interview customers. A leading question is when you ask a question that prompts a certain answer. Leading questions skew answers. The problem with leading questions, argues research experts at NN/g, is that:

> They interject the answer we want to hear in the question itself. They make it difficult or awkward for the participant to express another opinion… Leading questions result in biased or false answers, as respondents are prone to simply mimic the words of the interviewer.[2]

Let's look at a few examples of leading and neutral questions in Table 3.

Table 3: Examples of leading and neutral questions

Leading Questions	Neutral Questions
How annoying is it putting your kids to bed?	Tell me about the last time you put your child to bed.
How amazing was it to be shortlisted for business of the year award?	How do you feel about being shortlisted for business of the year award?
Isn't Christmas just like the best time of year?	What is your favourite time of year?
How relaxing is it to read fiction on holiday?	What do you do to relax on holiday?

---

[2] A. Schade, *Avoid leading questions to get better insights from participants*, Nielsen Norman Group (NN/g) (December 2017). Available from: www.nngroup.com/articles/leading-questions

Asking leading questions is easy to do and the only way to curb it is to be aware of it and check your questions before an interview. Let's take another fictional example.[3]

Your local post office is doing a bit of research about queuing. So many parcels are sent these days and waiting times are on the rise. Your local post office is trying to understand the customer waiting experience. A leading question could go like this: *How frustrating is it to wait in line at the post office?* In this question by using the word *frustrating* you are projecting your assumption about the customer's waiting experience and your interviewee might well go along with your interpretation even if it's not exactly true.

Is queuing at the post office frustrating? It depends. Are you in a hurry? Do you have kids in tow? Is your phone fully charged? Are you bursting for a pee (do NOT recommend). Let's say for a minute the post office reframed the question. *Tell me about what it's like to wait in line at the post office?* What could they find out?

Maybe the post office has no budget to address the actual problem of waiting in line (highly probable) and can't hire new staff. But by understanding how customers feel about waiting in line, I can think of a few different ways they could improve the waiting experience. Can you?

- Phone charging points along the queue
- Kids colouring station with branded colouring sheets and crayons
- Free water station
- Free Wi-Fi
- Accessible toilets

---

[3] Example originally inspired by *The ultimate guide to doing kickass customer interviews*, User Interviews. Available from: www.userinterviews.com/blog/the-ultimate-guide-to-doing-kickass-customer-interviews

Some people don't mind waiting in line. They relish the chance to scroll on their phone, catch up with some emails or listen to a podcast. Moral of the post office story, don't project assumptions onto your audience when asking them questions. Keep the language neutral and let customers describe their own personal experiences. You'll have more chance of getting to their truth.

3. Avoid hypothetical questions

Stop asking customers whether they're interested in your idea. I'm aware of how counterintuitive this sounds. I'm championing speaking to customers AND I'm telling you not to ask them whether they're interested in your product or service. These ideas can, and do, co-exist. Survey platform Smart Survey defines a hypothetical question as 'one based on supposition, not facts. They are typically used to elicit opinions and beliefs about imagined situations or conditions that don't exist.'[4]

In other words, the future. The future doesn't exist (yet). It's one of the biggest mistakes I see small businesses make. I did the research, they tell me, I asked them whether they were interested in my online course idea, and they said yes. But when I launched my course... nada.

That's probably because you were asking a hypothetical question: If I *were* to launch an online course about [insert as appropriate], would you be interested in buying it? Customers are likely to tell you what you want to hear. In other words, YES. Especially to small business owners. The proximity to customers, which comes from being a small business, works wonders for getting people to speak to you, but it doesn't guarantee they won't tell you porkies. In the *future*, customers have no skin in the game. 'Self-reported claims are unreliable, as

---

[4] Smart Survey, *Hypothetical questions*, smartsurvey.co.uk. Available from: www.smartsurvey.co.uk/survey-questions/hypothetical-questions

are user speculations about future behaviour,' as Jakob Nielsen founder of NN/g reminds us.[5] What should we ask instead?

The better questions to ask are those that uncover present and past behaviours. If you're still hung up on launching an online course, ask questions about whether they've taken an online course in the past. When was that? How much was it? Did they complete it? What did they get from it? What were the challenges? Even if someone says they have never bought an online course, find out whether they have considered it in the past, why didn't they buy in the end? By switching the focus of your questions from the future to the past and present, you'll be able to gather evidence (or not) on whether your customers are already displaying the behaviours and habits you need to see to be confident your course could work.

The discrepancy between what people say they'll do and what they do is called the intention-action gap. In her book *Continuous Discovery*, Teresa Torres gives a useful example. During a workshop, she asked a lady what factors she considered when buying a new pair of jeans:

> She didn't hesitate to answer. She said, 'Fit is my number-one factor.' I then asked her to tell me about the last time she bought a pair of jeans. She said, 'I bought them on Amazon.' I asked, 'How did you know they would fit?' She replied, 'I didn't but they were a brand I liked, and they were on sale.'[6]

Teresa says this workshop story is far from unique. She writes:

---

[5] J. Nielsen, *First rule of usability? Don't listen to users*, Nielsen Norman Group (NN/g) (August 2011). Available from: www.nngroup.com/articles/first-rule-of-usability-dont-listen-to-users
[6] T. Torres, *Continuous Discovery Habits*, Product Talk LLC, p.74 (2021).

I've asked people these same two questions countless times in workshops. The purchasing factors often vary, but there is always a gap between the first answer and the second. These participants aren't lying. We just aren't very good at understanding our own behaviour.[7]

Another behaviour with a fancy name: optimistic self-prediction. This is one to keep an eye on when testing out *virtuous* additions or developments to your services. Sustainability is a case in point. Investing in more sustainable production processes (sourcing organic ethical cotton for a new clothes line, for example) can be costly and may require passing at least some of the additional costs on to your customer.

At the heart of optimistic self-prediction is the notion that everyone is more virtuous in the future. While most people you ask will say they care about saving the planet from burning, in reality few put their money where their mouth is. Cost still remains one of the biggest drivers of choice for a lot of customers. In their article 'The Elusive Green Customer' for *The Harvard Business Review*, Katherine White, David J. Hardisty and Rishad Habib write 'a frustrating paradox remains at the heart of green business: Few consumers who report positive attitudes towards eco-friendly products and services follow through with their wallets.'[8]

We all do it. We are always healthier, smarter, greener and more organized in the future. So, whether it's the intention-action gap or our tendency for optimistic self-prediction, watch out. Keep your head and questions firmly in the present and the past. Business is not a zero-risk game but by avoiding

[7] T. Torres, *Continuous Discovery Habits*, Product Talk, LLC, p.75 (2021).
[8] K. White, D.J. Hardisty and R. Habib, 'The elusive green customer' for *Harvard Business Review* (July-August 2019). Available from: https://hbr.org/2019/07/the-elusive-green-consumer

hypothetical questions you'll at least get yourself closer to what that future reality *could* look like.

4. Use the toddler technique (five whys)

A why can get you far and five whys even further. This bona fide technique is used across a range of sectors. It identifies the root cause of more or less any problem. The five whys technique was originally developed by Sakichi Toyoda, the Japanese industrialist and founder of Toyota in the 1930s. While Sakichi was the first to develop this technique in a manufacturing context, kids have been asking why repetitively for like... ever. Us small businesses? Not enough. As we saw in Chapter 3, as we get older inhibitions take root and curiosity feels awkward. It takes some practice, but the toddler technique works absolute wonders and can be a fruitful way of generating new ideas.

A few years ago, I was presenting to a group of small creative business owners, waxing lyrical about the five whys technique and how it could transform their customer conversations. They were nodding enthusiastically. Then the facilitator put me on the spot. 'So, Katie, how would this work for Belinda?' she asked. Belinda runs Pothies, a creative business in Wales. Among other cosy delights, Belinda makes and sells crochet slippers. I asked the group to imagine Belinda was exploring new audiences for her slippers and had set up some interviews with potential new customers. I then demonstrated how the conversation could go one of two ways.

Conversation 1 (**without** toddler technique):

B: Hello, thanks so much for taking the time to speak to me today. My first question is do you own a pair of slippers?

Interviewee: No, actually I don't.

B: Ah ok, fair enough, I have a small slipper business and was doing some market research today, thanks so much, sorry for wasting your time, anyway, have a great day.

Now, let's look at Conversation 2 with the five whys technique in action. I have numbered the whys from 1–5 in the dialogue to show how B could get to the root cause.

<u>Conversation 2</u> (**with** toddler technique):

B: Hello, thanks so much for taking the time to speak to me today. I wanted to start by asking you whether you own a pair of slippers?

Interviewee: No, actually I don't.

B: Oh ok, that's interesting, why [#1] is that?

Interviewee: I used to but since I have got a dog, I stopped buying them.

B: Oh no, why [#2] is that?

Interviewee: Because he's chewed every single pair I've bought so far.

(Note: Belinda could give up now as she has found out one reason. But that was only two whys. Better to keep probing)

B: Tell me about it! Dogs love chewing slippers don't they? Why [#3] does your dog do that, do you think?

Interviewee: It's my fault really. I always leave them out at the bottom of the stairs before going to bed.

B: Perfect spot for the dog to find them! Is there any reason why [#4] you leave them out?

Interviewee: Well, we do have a shoe cupboard in the hallway but by the time we go to bed, there's no space left.

B: Sounds familiar, but tell me why [#5] is your shoe cupboard always so full?

Interviewee: We have three kids, and we have too many shoes.

B: I know exactly where you are coming from, I have three kids of my own.

What have we learnt here? This person doesn't own a pair of slippers but not because they don't like or want slippers.

What could Belinda do with this information? First, she could check whether this was the case for other pet owners. Then, if Belinda had budget for innovation, she could develop:

- Slippers with anti-chew rubber soles
- Dog repellent infused slipper fabric
- Protective slipper bag with handy adhesive hook for pet owners who can't cram any more footwear in the shoe cupboard (that's me too btw)
- A dog toy, shaped as a slipper, which comes with every purchase for a dog owner, to keep those gnawing jaws off the real deal.

But what if Belinda didn't have the budget to create anything brand new? Belinda could also keep it simple.

- A free dog treat for any dog owner buying a pair of your slippers with a playful message on the wrapper: *Eat me not the slipper*
- Print out fun stickers and slap them on your slippers: *We hope you love your slippers as much as your dog will. Keep them safe*

So many ideas by asking why five times. You might not always have the budget to solve all your customers' problems but acknowledging them can be the start of new opportunities. Innovation in business doesn't have to be costly, it can be just thoughtful. Thoughtful is underrated but hugely valuable.

From identifying barriers to people buying, to generating new ideas and improvements, the toddler technique will lead you to the root cause. Always use genuine curiosity and subtle cues to move the conversation along and dig a little deeper with each *why*.

5. Measuring joy and frustration.

In early 2022, I hit burnout. My body was screaming at me to slow down. Splitting headache and rock-hard shoulders and heart palpitations. I even went to A&E, convinced I was having a heart attack. I think it may be stress, the doctor told me. No shit.

The next morning, my personal trainer pulled her Theragun on me. She wrapped a towel around my neck. Told me to kneel and fired it up. The release was instant. I cried and went home. I turned on the laptop and I bought one. There and then: £175 on a massage contraption without batting an eyelid. Out of character? For sure.

People will pay if they care enough, if it hurts enough, delights enough and motivates enough. But how the hell do we measure enough?

Extract from Jungle Juice, 23rd May 2022

You can't improve what you can't measure, so we need to get better at measuring the messy stuff when we talk to customers. Asking quantifying questions helps because not all frustrations are created equal. Adam Forbes is programme director at Startupbootcamp. He told me:

When I work with business owners, I always start by asking them about the emotional state of their customer. They nearly always say 'they're frustrated'... We're all frustrated. Hell, I spend my life frustrated – but I only act on a small fraction of those frustrations.

Think about it. How many things vex you on a day-to-day basis? From minor inconveniences (where the hell is my phone?) to full blown I want to tear my hair out frustrations (trying to get an appointment with the doctor on a Monday morning after a bank holiday weekend). But I've yet to purchase one of those find my phone gadgets, nor have I resorted to private health care.

So, while your product or service certainly does need to solve a pain (or fulfil a need or desire), even a hearty 'this really pisses me off' shouldn't be confused with a strong buying signal. As Adam says, there are lots of things that are inconvenient, annoying pains in the backside. But the question is: which ones will we pay to fix? 'It's about both the acuteness of the pain and the urgency with which it needs to be fixed,' Adam added.

Nana Parry is an entrepreneur and founder of the customer research agency Tectonic. He co-founded his agency after his first business failed, primarily due to not understanding his customers. Nana created a platform to help independent musicians promote themselves more effectively. He spotted an opportunity to support them in uploading their music and mixes to multiple platforms in one click. He assumed it was a bit of a pain to upload music content to one platform, then have to do it all again for multiple other platforms. He knew the music scene well and interviewed a few music artists to make sure his assumption was correct. They agreed. So far so good. Nana and his team went away. They fixed that problem. They built a cool piece of tech. But nobody used it.

What went wrong? Nana recognized that while it was a pain for them to upload to multiple platforms, it was far from the

BIGGEST pain in their working lives. He eventually found out that a lot of independent musicians and DJs don't create new music that they are happy to release publicly that often. 'It wasn't taking a significant enough amount of time to upload to individual platforms. The problem just wasn't big enough,' Nana told me. He added: 'If we would have spent a bit more time understanding the frequency that music and mixes were created, I may not have spent money and burnt cash to build a feature that was effectively useless.'

Eventually after a few similar scenarios, Nana and his team walked away. They had a start-up, investors and a product but customers were not sticking around. He reflected:

> I realized that understanding customers is the most important part of starting a business. I spent way too much time learning about product development, how to build features, how to raise money. It was a harsh awakening. If I don't have paying customers, I don't have a business.

These days, his agency Tectonic helps clients avoid the same fate.

In my research for clients, I centre my quantifying questions around four main areas. You should too. You want to measure:

- Frustration (How painful?)
- Time (How long? How often?)
- Money (How much?)
- Success (What does it look like?)

By digging deep across these areas, you'll get a better idea of whether your offer solves a big enough pain (as in one a customer will pay to alleviate) or fulfils a big enough need or desire (again, one a customer cares enough about to pay). We need to get better at picking up strong buying signals and weeding out the weaker ones by asking more quantifying questions.

Let's dwell on success for a moment. How customers define success (has the *job* – as in JTBD – they set out to do, been done successfully?) is nebulous, subjective and slippery. How *do* we measure success? How do we measure what good looks like for our customers? Success is wound up in expectations and customer satisfaction and can be quantified to an extent with the right questions. As with frustrations, not all successes are equal. For example, your bank card working in your local Tesco is a success but not a special one, you wouldn't pay extra for that feature because it's inherently part of the product (a bank card works when you need it). If you were setting up a new bank, you wouldn't wax lyrical about your bank card working in Tesco. It's a given.

Let's look at what success does and doesn't look like for a customer in the following fictional (and close to my heart) example.

You run an e-commerce business selling kids' clothes. You want to expand your range and reach new audiences. You've been doing some research and have read that the adaptive apparel (clothes that are adaptable in case of a physical disability or neurodivergence) market was worth $300 billion in 2021 and set to grow another 16% by 2023.[9] Fertile ground to help underserved people and grow your business. You narrow it down to the idea of launching a new sensory-friendly kids' clothes range (think soft seams to virtually seamless, no labels, soft and tight-fitting fabrics). Kids with sensory challenges tend to be very particular with how clothes feel, and you had evidence to suggest that parents struggle to find sensory-friendly clothes that match the design variety of non-sensory clothes.

---

[9] Global adaptive apparel market size from 2019 to 2024 (December 2022). Available from www.statista.com/statistics/875613/global-adaptive-apparel-market-size/

You assume, before interviewing parents, that success would equal having a greater variety of designs to choose from as the current offering is restrictive (think more patterns, prints and colour options). You've diligently read *Do Penguins Eat Peaches?* and set up interviews with target parents. Throughout the course of these conversations, you realize something else completely. In fact, you learn that success is less about having a wider range of sensory-friendly clothes (although that would be a welcome plus) but how flexible the returns policy is. Sensory kids tend to take much longer to accept new clothes (talking from direct experience over here!). As a parent you can't immediately tell if your child will wear a new item of clothing or not. They often need a period of time to get over the newness, and to do this they need to be able to wear the clothes and try them out. This process can take anything from a few days to a few weeks. It's often a painful cycle of cutting off the price tag, the child trying it on, rejecting it, and then trying it on again. The story normally ends one of two ways. Your kid finally accepts it (success), or they don't (more pain). But because it's been weeks since you bought it, the price tag has been cut off and it's been worn (albeit only once for 20 seconds max). You're in breach of all return policy rules.

Armed with this information, you could launch your new range with several innovative solutions to support struggling parents. These could include:

- An extended, more flexible return window
- A 'try before you buy' scheme
- A resell platform for parents with piles of unworn clothes at the back of the wardrobe

In this example, we found evidence of customers already spending money trying to fix their problem but not finding much success. This is always fertile ground for businesses. Never assume what pain and success look like for customers. Ask instead.

Quantifying questions

Here are a few helpful questions to start you off on your quest to measure frustration and success (you'll find them again in the Question Bank at the back of this book).

- How long does it normally take you to…?
- How frequently do you have to do it?
- How much time would you ideally like to spend on it?
- Which is the most frustrating part of doing…?
- How does that compare to the other frustrations you've mentioned when doing…?
- How are you currently solving this problem?
- How much money do you currently spend on solving this problem?
- What are your thoughts on the amount you currently spend on solving this problem?
- What is the most rewarding part of doing….?
- What does success look like when you…?
- What does good look like when you…?

Top tip: If the person you're asking responds 'it depends' to one of your quantifying questions, throw them a bone. Let's say you're asking how long it takes them to do their monthly accounts and your customer says it depends. Follow up with options: 'I understand but would you say it normally takes a few days or a few weeks?' If the ranges you suggest are roomy enough, you'll be sure to get a better answer. 'Oh no! Not that long, it normally takes me a few hours.' Bingo.

In addition to asking quantifying questions in your interviews, ask customers to rank any frustrations they mention from 1–5, 1 being the most urgent and painful frustration. This also works well when you're trying to get a handle on what customer success looks like.

To sum up

Customers go about their lives trying to get stuff done (jobs), and to do so they seek out a number of different products and services. They choose products and services not only because they fulfil a functional use (tell the time, wipe your butt) but because they also fulfil emotional and social needs (make me look good, make me feel good). It's your job as a small business owner to ask good questions (by sticking to my five golden rules) and plough all the juicy stuff you find out back into your business. Peachy. So next time you pull together a customer conversation guide, no more stupid questions. Deal? Once you have a bunch of interviews in the bag, have all your notes and transcripts, you need to make sense of it all. In research circles, we call it sensemaking. It requires a bit of (colourful) kit and time, but it isn't half as painful as it sounds.

Chapter 5 recap:

- JTBD helps you understand what *jobs* customers are trying to get done.

- JTBD helps you understand what drives customer behaviour (not just functional needs but emotional and social too).

- JTBD reframes how you see your competitors.

- Ask open-ended questions to get customers to share stories.

- Avoid leading questions, instead use neutral language.

- Avoid hypothetical questions, instead stick to questions about past and present behaviours.

- Ask why five times to get to the root cause.

- Where possible, quantify customer joy and frustration.

6 The art and science of sensemaking

I spent hours in the classroom trying to make sense of what the teacher was saying. I was 10, English and surrounded by French school kids.

I'd crossed the channel a few weeks prior. UK house sold. French house bought. Our Charleston 2CV filled to the brim, cat, and all.

Our French adventure was about to begin…

Those early weeks, I kept one eye on the teacher and the other on my musty yellow and blue *Teach Yourself French* book.

Learning a new language is a sensemaking game. Finding patterns, forming hypotheses and then one day, things start to make sense.

Making sense of what customers tell you is a similar game. A more conscious one, sure, but a similar game nonetheless.

Extract from Jungle Juice, 24th April 2023

Customer interviews, even if you follow a discussion guide, are by nature messy. The answers you get are unstructured thoughts, feelings and opinions, straight out of someone's mouth. Words and phrases unique to that person's way of describing things. It makes it harder to measure than the responses you'd get from a tidy survey (e.g. 85% of respondents said penguins don't eat peaches). But it's doable. In this chapter, I'll guide you through a few methods you can use to bring a little process and rigour to making sense of your customer conversations.

What is sensemaking?

Figuring out what all the stuff you've heard means is an important part of your market research process. We call it sensemaking. Travis Lowdermilk and Jessica Rich in their book *The Customer-Driven Playbook* describe it as 'a process that ensures we organize the data we collect, identify patterns and meaningful insights.'[1] What's the point of intentionally talking to customers if we're not going to spend some time figuring out what it means? Sensemaking looks for repeatable ideas, behaviours and themes in our interviews. Let's say you want to create a product helping people to achieve their daily recommended water intake. Your hypothesis and premise for this idea is that *a majority of people struggle to drink the required daily amount of water.* You do 10 interviews. Sensemaking would be the process of going from 10 interview transcripts to something you can measure better (e.g. eight out of ten people I spoke to said they struggled to keep hydrated through the day). If you've never done it before, sensemaking requires a bit

---

[1] T. Lowdermilk and J. Rich, *The Customer-Driven Playbook: Converting Customer-Driven Feedback into Successful Products*, O'Reilly Media, p. 47 (2017).

of guidance and time. But it must be done. Skipping this bit is tempting but a good enough approach is all you need.

Why do we need it?

First, our memories aren't reliable (I can't even remember what I had for dinner last night, you?). If we don't make some early sense of what we've heard, we'll forget. Waste of everyone's time. 'After you've conducted a handful of interviews… interviews will start to blur together. You don't want to rely on your memory to keep your research straight,' says Teresa Torres.[2]

Second, the whole point of interviewing customers is so we can understand them better and make evidence-based decisions for our business. If we don't intentionally spend time processing what we've heard, it'll make it hard to make any decision, let alone a good one.

Third, sometimes we park things and come back to them later. You might learn things from customers you were not expecting, things you may want to pick back up and explore later. As someone who can't read her handwriting a week later (let alone after a few months), it makes sense to get things in some kind of order before tucking it away for future use. Finally, if at some point you need to involve other people in your business (consultants, coaches, freelancers…) or have ambitions to grow your team, having your customer insight in a format others can look at and make sense of can only be a good thing.

When to do it?

Sensemaking ideally happens in two phases. The first phase is immediately after an interview. Spend 10–15 minutes

---

[2] T. Torres, *Continuous Discovery Habits*, Product Talk LLC, p. 84 (2021).

doing some housekeeping and make a note of anything that immediately jumps out at you. Think of it as tidying up as you go along instead of being faced with a big mess come the weekend. This phase can be lightweight. For example, go through any manual notes you made and highlight anything noteworthy. Save the interview recording in a safe place (by safe I mean where you can *actually* find it a week later), generate a transcript, skim read it and highlight anything noteworthy (as I've mentioned before, I use Grain but there are other tools out there).

Creating an interview snapshot also works well in this first phase. It's basically a one-page document where you quickly capture what you've learnt from an interview. You jot down key information from your discussion which helps jog your memory when you get to the second sensemaking part. Teresa Torres has developed her own one-pager that might work for you too. The snapshot has a visual (a picture of the person or a picture that reminds you of them based on something they said), a memorable quote, some quick facts (essentially demographics), key insights (or learnings) and what she calls opportunities (a need, pain point or a desire expressed during the interview). Teresa explains:

> The goal with a snapshot is to capture as much of what you heard in each interview as possible. It's easy to discount a behaviour as unique to a particular participant, but you should still capture what you heard in the interview snapshot... You'll be surprised at how often an opportunity that seems unique to customers becomes a common pattern heard in several interviews.[3]

---

[3] T. Torres, *Continuous Discovery Habits*, Product Talk LLC, p. 86 (2021).

Phase two of the sensemaking phase is when you've finished all your interviews and are ready to identify patterns, trends and repeatable ideas. This takes half a day to a day, depending on the number of interviews you've done. If you cannot afford to spend that time in one go, split it over two sessions. This may sound a lot but it's worthwhile, business-changing work. Remember what you'll learn can save you time, money and tears down the line. If you think you don't have time, check your phone usage (works for me every time).

As soon as you have some interviews scheduled in the diary (ideally over a two-week period), open your calendar and schedule the sensemaking session (or two split sessions). You're unlikely to have a chock-a-block diary three to four weeks out so it will be easier to allocate the time. If you don't work with online calendars, use a diary or however else you manage your time. Don't have that either? Maybe (just maybe) this would be a good time to start. Colour coding optional.

What you need

- **A digital shoebox.** If you want to keep all your nuggets warm you need to build an oven, a place to put all your recordings, transcripts and notes. If you work mainly solo, a folder on your computer will do. Want a bit more security? Save them in an online folder (e.g. Google Drive). Either way, password protect the data.
- **Notepad.** Ideally one pad for all the interview notes you take. If you are not that organized (like me) your everyday scruffy notepad works fine too.
- **Highlighter.** So many hues to choose from these days. I'd stick to the classics, bold and bright, so stuff you highlight *actually* stands out. Buy new or steal from a school child in your life. Or if you are the digital type, highlight on your screen.

- **Sticky notes**. Your brand of choice of course. I know my favourite (my top tip on how to peel a sticky note off for maximum wall adhesion on request).
- **Wall**. Somewhere you can stick your notes (ideally where little hands or furry paws won't tear them down as soon as your back is turned).
- **Printer**. I'm old-school and like to print out the transcripts (use recycled paper where possible). On-screen might work well for you. Your choice.
- **Excel**. Really NOT my favourite place to hang out, but brilliant for organizing data, patterns and themes.
- **Time**. Do not underestimate the power of putting two hours of sensemaking in your calendar, three weeks in advance. Business owners who plan in deep work are more likely to feel on top of things and run successful businesses. Stop resisting (I see you).
- **A business buddy** (optional). Why not ask a business bestie to join you. Fresh pair of unbiased eyes on your transcripts and all that jazz.
- **Snacks**. Lots of them.

How to do it

Making sense of qualitative data (words) is part science, part art. The key is to bring just enough rigour to enable you to draw conclusions. In this next section, I'll share two different ways you could do it. There are other methods out there, but they all boil down to the same thing: finding repeatable ideas, patterns and trends that can help you make decisions. The method you settle on will depend on the time you have, what type of interviews you did and how your brain prefers to work. Remember a blend of both approaches works well too.

Hypothesis tracking

First up, the hypothesis tracking method. Loved by start-ups for its laser-sharp properties, it will suit those of you doing short, regular bursts of customer discovery. If the main purpose of your interview is to prove or disprove an assumption, this method ticks the boxes. You'll end up with something you can measure, something quantifiable (especially useful if you're trying to get funding or persuade other people you have found a real problem).

Adam Forbes from Startupbootcamp favours this method. He told me:

> The broad questions are good for customer interviews. You get loads on insight and information you can feed into the next round of research, but I think in each customer interview at least 50% of your time should be focused on testing those two to four hypotheses you have.

Let's try it on our water business example from the beginning of this chapter. Imagine you've completed 10 interviews. Table 4 shows us hypothesis tracking in practice.

Table 4: Hypothesis method example

My hypotheses	Yes = 1	No = 0
Most people don't drink their recommended daily intake of water	1, 1, 1, 1, 1, 1, 1, 1	0, 0
Most people don't know what their daily recommended water intake should be	1, 1, 1, 1, 1	0, 0, 0, 0, 0
Most people want to drink the recommended amount	1, 1, 1, 1, 1, 1	0, 0, 0, 0

It's a checklist. Every time you hear your customer say something that ether validates or disproves your hypothesis, you write a '1' for yes and a '0' for no. You can use this type of table as a framework to make sense of your interview notes. As you get more confident, you can do it in real time as you are speaking to customers. Excel is your friend with this method and over time (and interviews) enables you to visualize your findings (tables and graphs, pivot tables if you're feeling fancy).

Here is a quick summary of the pros and cons of tracking hypotheses:

Pros: Easy to quantify; suits shorter, targeted interviews.

Cons: Could miss other useful information including context and adjacent customer challenges.

Affinity mapping

Next, affinity mapping. This method works well after exploratory interviews (the higher-level interviews we explored in Chapter 4). You may be fishing for new ideas, trying to understand customer behaviours and habits or exploring challenges customers have in certain areas of their lives. With this method, you go through each interview (transcript/notes) and every time you find a noteworthy idea, you write it on a sticky note. One idea per sticky note. Write down the initials of the person you spoke to at the top of the sticky note for reference (or anonymize with Customer 1, 2, 3, etc.). At this stage, go with your gut. Don't overthink it because you risk spiralling into endless doubt about whether the idea is interesting or not. Just write it down and stick it up on the wall (if you don't have the wall space you can try an online, virtual tool such as Miro).

Once you've been through your interview transcripts and notes, look at all your sticky notes on the wall/floor (or leave it until your next sensemaking session if you're doing it over two days). Then start grouping them by themes (themes will emerge!). At the end of the process, you'll have some clear groupings with repeatable ideas and themes. Don't forget to take a picture of all your sticky notes (just in case they fall, or small hands and/or muddy paws tear them down when you're not looking).

Sara Fortier runs a service design agency Outwitly in Canada. She is a big fan of this method and told me:

> Affinity mapping is one of the most approachable ways to make sense of everything you've heard. Smaller businesses shouldn't be scared off by it, nor should they overthink it. Remember you're not reporting to a head of insight or writing a research paper for an academic journal, you're just trying to see whether you can see any patterns in what your audience has told you.

Here is a quick summary of the pros and cons of affinity mapping:

Pros: Great for visual learners, helps identify adjacent insights and opportunities.

Cons: Need wall space, more time intensive.

Back to our water business. Over the next few pages, you'll find three fictional interview transcripts. I've highlighted (using bold and italics) some of the repeatable ideas across the three. I've then grouped them into themes to give you a sense of what this method looks like in practice.

Interview 1: Joy | Female | 44

How much water did you drink yesterday?
Not enough. I probably drank one bottle, which is about 75cl I think. I kept thinking I needed to refill it but between meetings, the kids and the dog it just never happened.

How do you feel about that amount?
It's not enough, I know that much. I really want to drink more but life is so busy.

How much water would you like to be drinking per day?
Ideally at least one litre. I do manage it sometimes.

How much water is recommended per day?
I'm never too sure. Depends on what article you read but I think it's two litres? Does that include teas and other liquids? To be honest, it's hard to keep track of water intake unless you're drinking from the same bottle every time.

What have you done in the past to try to drink more water?
I've tried buying different kinds of water bottles. I find transparent bottles the most useful because you can see what you're drinking. *I've tried buddying up* with my partner to see whether we can remind each other to drink more throughout the day. *I've set reminders on my phone* too.

Interview 2: Ayesha | Female | 39

How much water did you drink yesterday?
Probably about one and a half litres.

How do you feel about that amount?
I know how important it is to drink more. Everyone is always saying drink more, drink more. When I do, I feel less sluggish.

How much water would you like to be drinking per day?
If I could at least get to a consistent one and a half litres I would be on to a good start. Not sure I'm ready for two litres or more just yet. I'm struggling to get to one litre at the moment.

How much water is recommended per day?
Between two and three litres I think? Every time I read something about it it's in fluid ounces or glasses, it's confusing.

What have you done in the past to try and drink more water?
I've tried leaving a bottle in different locations. If I have a desk day, I'm more likely to hit it as I am not moving about so much. If I am working, running errands, walking with the dog, picking up the kids I don't always remember to bring my water bottle everywhere. But the problem with that is when you're drinking from different bottles you never remember how much you drank in total.

Interview 3: David | Male | 43

How much water did you drink yesterday?
I'm not quite sure. A bit more than usual because I did a workout. Probably about three glasses with meals and a bottle at the gym so maybe one and a half litres or something like that.

How do you feel about that amount?
Um... okay, I guess. Ideally, I'd be drinking a bit more. I'm trying to drink two litres a day but it's not always easy to keep track of how much I drink. Most days it's probably more like one litre.

How much water would you like to be drinking per day?
As I said, I'm aiming for two litres but it's a struggle. And my fancy water bottle isn't even one litre, probably more like 75cl. It also depends on what my day looks like. If I'm at my desk, I can keep track better but come the weekend I always drink less because I'm out and about.

How much water is recommended per day?
Is it two litres? Or maybe it's three litres? Do you know what, I don't actually know, and does it change depending on your age?

What have you done in the past to try and drink more water?
I've tried an app in the past. The reminders were useful but all they said was 'remember to drink.' But if I'm not near my water bottle and I'm busy, I will ignore it. I've also tried *putting a bottle next to my bed* so I can drink first thing in the morning.

Here is an example of what the start of our affinity mapping could look like for our water interviews. I have identified two themes for this example. What other patterns have you spotted?

Theme 1: Confusing drinking guidance (see quotes underlined from the interviews)

Joy	**Ayesha**	**David**
'I'm never too sure'; 'Does it include teas and other liquids?'; 'It's hard to keep track'	'Every time I read something about it... It's confusing.'	'I don't actually know... does it change depending on your age?'

Theme 2: Intent or evidence of wanting to drink more (quotes in italics from the interviews)

Joy	**Ayesha**	**David**
'I've tried buying different kinds of water bottles'; 'I've tried buddying up'; 'Set reminders on my phone.'	'I've tried leaving bottles in different locations.'	'I've tried an app... [and] putting water next to my bed.'

Outliers

When interviewing customers, you're bound to get a few curve balls. An idea or an opinion that doesn't align with what else you've been hearing. In maths, we call them outliers. They tend to stick out like a sore thumb. Discard them from your sensemaking unless it's an interesting enough idea to investigate later. When it comes to outliers, Sara from Outwitly has more advice for us:

> You don't want to skew all your data based on something that only one person said, but sometimes there is value in what one person said, especially when there is a lot of passion behind it. It might be interesting enough to come back to.

Outliers are easy to spot amongst a dozen or so customer interviews but are more difficult to spot when in isolation. Remember, it's possible the feedback you receive directly and unsolicited from one customer could be an outlier. Check.

Finally, just because we are self-employed or running small businesses, it does not make us exempt from data protection rules and guidelines. Protecting your customers' data is important. Be sure to check out the guidance in Chapter 13. In the meantime, a few tips:

- Anonymize your interviews as much as possible
- Save your recordings and transcripts in a secure location (password protected)
- Dispose of them once they are no longer needed (less important if they are anonymized)
- Make sure your customer knows the purpose of the interview
- Get consent to record the interview before the interview

To sum up

Sensemaking is an essential part of making the most of your customer conversations. Make time for it and do it with just enough rigour and you *will* find patterns in your data that can power your next move. Just make sure you're asking the same questions (give or take) for each round of interviews so you can compare like for like. Interviews are the holy grail when it comes to understanding customers but there are plenty of other research methods to play with as a small business. In our next chapter, we'll look at surveys. Surveys are popular, quick and cheap. They are also overused and fraught with danger, as we are about to find out.

Chapter 6 recap:

- Sensemaking is part art, part science (we're looking at just enough rigour for it to be useful).

- Don't skip this step. Schedule in the time, in advance.

- Affinity mapping and hypothesis tracking are two ways you can use to make sense of what customers are telling you.

- Be mindful of data protection rules and guidelines (for more information see Chapter 13).

- Keep your ego in check. Even at this stage it's still easy to slip into seeing and hearing what we want to believe to be true.

- A bonus of sensemaking is gathering evidence on how your customer speaks and what language they use (useful for writing marketing copy).

7 Stop sending shitty surveys

Sent a survey to your customers yet? Got one in the works? Is it on your must-get-around-to-probably-won't-have-time-maybe-next-month list? (I have one of those too.)

Online surveys are easy to set up and SO easy to get wrong. Biggest survey blunder? Surveys without purpose. For the sake of it.

There are loads of other things we should do for the sake of it. Taking a walk in the sunshine, taking up a new hobby we enjoy (even if we suck at it) and staring at the flames of an open fire. Just because. But surveys aren't one of them.

Extract from Jungle Juice, 27th February 2023

Businesses use surveys a lot. Too much, says Erika Hall. 'Surveys are the most dangerous and misused of all potential research tools or methods in the realm of doing things online... surveys are really overused, badly used, and people should mostly just stop.'[1] Ouch. In this chapter we'll

---

[1] E. Hall interviewed by Carrie Boyd, *Awkward Silences* podcast by User Interviews, Episode 21 (July 2019). Available from: www.userinterviews.com/blog/erika-hall-on-why-surveys-almost-always-suck

look at what exactly is a survey, when to use them and how to create a really good one.

What is a survey?

A survey is what we call a quantitative research method (as opposed to a qualitative method such as customer interviews). You gather responses to predefined questions from a specific group of people. Responses you can quantify. Most surveys are done either in person, over the phone or online. A survey feels easy, too easy. You often don't need to speak to anyone and barriers to setting one up are low but creating a good survey is deceivingly hard. Bad survey questions lead to bad data and bad data lead to bad decisions. If you think about it, surveys by nature only give you a slice of your customer's reality, the one elicited by the predefined list of questions you ask. That said, surveys can still be a very useful tool for small businesses if you know how to create good ones.

When should you use a survey?

Whether or not you decide to use a survey will depend on what you're trying to find out. If not, don't ask anyone for anything until you do. Put some thought into it or hire in some help (see Chapter 13). Otherwise, it's a waste of everyone's time.

Surveys are the right method to use when you are:

- Gathering demographics data to determine your audience (e.g. age, gender, nationality, residence, education, profession…).
- Understanding behaviours. Zooming in on one or two customer behaviours and habits you want to learn more about.
- Capturing in-the-moment feedback (e.g. in a shop, an airport, a restaurant, on your website).

- Validating hypotheses and assumptions on a bigger scale (this can be useful after a round of customer interviews).
- Evaluating customer satisfaction after a product/service has been delivered.

Build surveys people fill in

Once you know what you want to find out, you need some questions. The rules are different for surveys than for customer interviews, especially online. People are goldfishes online. If you want them to fill in your survey, you need to craft questions carefully. There's plenty written on the types of questions you can ask: the pros and cons of multiple choice, Likert scales and whatnot. Survey platforms spend a lot of time educating businesses on survey question mechanics. Super-important stuff but don't get carried away debating what type of question will elicit the best response before getting some fundamentals in place. You're not Ipsos, but you can probably improve on what you're doing now.

Keep your surveys tight with these top 10 tips:

1. **Be human**. How hard can that be? From the number of robotic surveys I've seen, harder than you think. I've seen the most humorous, warm, friendly and chatty people turn into robots the moment they write survey questions. Write as you speak. Nobody goes around asking people *What is your country of residence?* So, unless you work in border control, ask *Where do you live?* instead. Reading questions out loud helps spot robotic tendencies. A survey is a conversation, a structured one, but a conversation, nonetheless. Whether you're selling finance software to middle managers or mittens to vegans, be friendly and on the right side of chatty. Pay attention to the transition copy between questions.

How your survey flows can make all the difference.

2. **Stick (mostly) to closed questions**. By closed questions I mean a question that can be answered by yes or no. Or by clicking an option on a multiple choice list. People want to get through the survey as quickly as possible. Nobody is hoping for a long survey. By all means, pepper your survey with a few open-ended questions (a question you cannot answer by simply yes or no) but make sure they are strategically placed. There is nothing worse than clicking on a survey and finding the first question gives you brain ache: *To what extent did Brexit have an impact on your mental health?* Cue, exit survey. You've lost them. A good survey is like a banging tune, it has a rhythm to it. If you're going to elicit some responses from open-ended questions, make sure there are some easy-to-answer questions before it. Warm people up. As a rule, no more than two open-ended questions per 10 questions.

3. **Number of questions**. The shorter the better. Seven to ten questions is the sweet spot for customer surveys (you can go shorter for pulse surveys, which will be three to four questions max on a more regular basis). A 10-question survey takes about five minutes for people to fill in. After that, it's a game of diminishing returns. Research shows that the longer the survey, the quicker people fill it in (think race through the second half because they've already lost the will to live). It's called satisficing. Also, don't make every question mandatory (they HAVE to answer it before they can move on). It puts people off, especially if there's a question a respondent wants to skip. Identify the core questions you really need responses to and toggle accordingly (most survey platforms have this option).

4. **Embrace smart multiple choice**. Don't make your respondent think too much. Instead of *When thinking*

about my brand what words come to mind? And then leaving an open space, make a list of words and then add *Other* with a box if they want to add something specific. Always think, how can I make this easy for the person filling in the survey? The less thinking for them, the better.

5. **Don't ask if you won't act**. It's best practice in research not to ask questions if you are not going to do anything with the responses. Curiosity for curiosity's sake? Not in surveys.

6. **Think beyond the survey**. Always use a survey as a recruitment tool for customer interviews. Throw in a tick box at the end with something along the lines of *We are always looking for customers to talk to further about our products and services, if you would like to be contacted in the future, please tick this box* (amend as necessary).

7. **Incentivize**. Everyone loves a freebie. Without breaking the bank, think about what you could do to sweeten the deal. A prize draw can work well for smaller sample sizes. Be creative but don't be afraid of trying your luck without (more incentive ideas back in Chapter 4).

8. **Other**. If you don't embrace smart multiple choice (see point 4) it's highly likely that you'll get lots of *Other* responses (because you don't know what you don't know and all that). So do everyone a favour and add a box for free text so you can learn what *Other* means.

9. **Test**. I'm no spelling bee but in the 21st century there aren't many excuses not to check. Get your prose on point. Test for flow and typos before you press send. After a basic spell-check, rope in friends and family (the only time I'll allow it). Ask them to fill it in. You'll be surprised at what a fresh pair of eyes will find.

10. **Explain and empathize**. You're asking for their precious time. Acknowledge and appreciate it. Tell them why you're doing it and what you're going to do with

what you find out. You don't have to go into all the details but offering up a little behind the scenes can really help get people supporting your survey.

Work backwards

If you are struggling to word your survey questions to ask, Erika Hall recommends working back from the type of responses that would be useful to get from your audience.[2] For example, imagine you are a Virtual Assistant (VA) exploring whether your existing clients would buy VA admin holiday cover. A useful survey outcome in your quest to decide whether this is something your clients would be interested could be: 75% of my customers went on holiday abroad at least once last year. The question would therefore be: *How many times did you holiday abroad last year?* As you can appreciate, that response alone is certainly not enough to launch your new holiday cover service and plenty of other questions would need to be asked. But if the response was that only 5% of your customers went on holiday abroad at least once last year, that might stop your idea in its tracks.

Your Question Bank (see Chapter 3) is another good place to start when establishing the goal of your survey. Look at the questions you've deposited. Are there any themes you can group together to try to find the answers to with a survey? One of the biggest mistakes I see with small business surveys is covering too many topics and goals in one survey. Keep your surveys tight and focused as it increases your chances of getting results you can act upon.

---

[2] E. Hall, *Just Enough Research* (2nd edition), A Book Apart, p. 145 (2019).

Make something happen

You've done the survey and you have some responses. Now do something already. How many times have I filled in surveys, either in person or online, and nothing happens. Zilch. A recent study by global consultancy McKinsey[3] showed that survey fatigue (not filling in surveys or filling them in sloppily) among employees in large companies was in fact less driven by the frequency and length of surveys but more by the sinking feeling that nothing would change. In other words, their responses didn't count. That's exactly how I feel. I fill in surveys for the brands and organizations I like but my willingness to continue is eroding. Filling in surveys these days feels like pissing in the wind. You click submit, your responses fly out into the metaverse, you never win the prize draw they lured you in with, and you never get a follow-up email to say what they did with your answers. What you do get is another *We'd love to hear your thoughts* email, six months later. We can do better than that.

This is where you take full advantage of small. Because behind the scenes things will inevitably be shifting after you look at the responses. Decisions will be made (great I can move to the next stage of my holiday VA idea) and hopes dashed (this idea is unlikely to work). And sometimes the responses will generate more questions than answers (time to do some customer interviews!). Tell people. Not every single detail but be *more* transparent than you are now. *You said, we did* messages build connections. It's powerful to show your audience their voice counts, that they matter. If your survey is tight, with a goal and good questions, there should always be a next step.

---

[3] A. DiLeonardo, T. Lauricella and B. Schaninger, *Survey fatigue? Blame the leader, not the question*, McKinsey (May 2021). Available from: www.mckinsey.com/capabilities/people-and-organizational-performance/our-insights/the-organization-blog/survey-fatigue-blame-the-leader-not-the-question

Sample sizes and response rates

Survey sample sizes are statistics on steroids (try saying that fast!). You can make it as simple or as complicated as you wish. The sample size is essentially the total number of responses you'll need to ensure your survey is statistically relevant. There are a few key metrics that matter when it comes to figuring out your sample size:

1. The confidence level or how accurate you want the survey to be. Rule of thumb, you want to be aiming for at least 90% confidence rate (95% ideally).
2. Your margin of error. For this metric, we're aiming for no lower than 10% (ideally 5%).
3. Total population size is the final number you need, or the number of people in total in the group you are studying.

How do you figure out your sample size? You don't, not by yourself anyway. As I mentioned in Chapter 2, Survey Monkey has a free online tool[4] that does all the heavy lifting for you. You input your confidence level and your margin of error. Next, you will need to set that total population number (a Google search can help you figure that out).

Here is an example using the Survey Monkey tool. Imagine you create a survey aimed at the LGBTQ+ community in the UK, that's about 1.5 million people.[5] If you set a 95% confidence level and a margin of error of 5%, according to Survey Monkey's sample size calculator, you'd need 385 people

---

4 Survey Monkey, *Sample size calculator*, surveymoney.co.uk. Available from: www.surveymonkey.co.uk/mp/sample-size-calculator
5 Office for National Statistics (ONS), *Sexual Orientation Census 2021*, ons.gov.uk. Available from: www.ons.gov.uk/peoplepopulationandcommunity/culturalidentity/sexuality

to respond to it for it to be statistically relevant. What does that mean in practice?

Let's say one of your survey questions was: Do you feel represented in mainstream media? and 60% of your respondents say no. In this instance, you can be 95% confident (your selected confidence level) that if you'd asked every person in the LGBTQ+ community that same question between 55% and 65% (60% plus or minus your percentage point margin of error, set at 5%) would have the same answer.

Then you need to think about completion rates. Average online survey completion rates range from 15% to 30% depending on a number of factors (e.g. survey length, question complexity and audience type). A 30% completion rate means out of every 100 people you send your survey to, only thirty will fill it all in. For our LGBTQ+ survey, we'd need to send it to approximately 1,283 people to ensure we hit our recommended 385 sample size (385 is 30% of 1,283). However, if you're sending a survey to get feedback and insights from your existing customer base, then (sample) size doesn't matter.

One last thing about sample sizes, make sure you have a screener question before the survey starts, as you want to ensure the people filling it in are in your target market. Botching up your sample is no fun. The example Jane Frost CBE and CEO of the MRS shared with me is a case in point. In 2016, employee benefits company My Family Care, and the Women's Business Council jointly published a survey claiming fewer than 1% of men had taken up the then newly introduced paternity leave option offered by employers. Media outlets across the UK covered the story. *Why the hell weren't men taking up this option to be with their new-borns?* was a popular news angle. Then journalist, author and broadcaster Tim Halford poked his nose into the data for his *More or Less* show on BBC Radio 4, and a whole different story came to light.[6] It transpired that the 1% being bandied around was, in fact, 1% of ALL men whether they'd fathered a baby over the last year or not. It changed everything. Remember, what you get out of a survey is only ever as good as what you put in. Same goes for cake and coffee. In this example, a simple screener question such as *Have you had a baby over the last 12 months?* would have done the job quite nicely.

Which platforms to use?

There are plenty of survey platforms to choose from and seasoned surveyors will have their favourites. Here are some of the most well-known and easy to use platforms for small businesses. Remember to always check what data protection laws (e.g. GDPR for the European Union) apply to your survey.

- **Google Forms**. Free version; easy to use; unlimited surveys and responses; limited response analytics; limited design features.
- **Survey Monkey**. User-friendly for novices and pros alike; provides lots of (written) support and guidance on best practice; good response analytics; restrictions on free version.
- **Type Form**. Stylish; easy to use; all about the user experience (for you and your respondents).
- **Zoho Surveys**. Advanced survey analytics; offline versions; brilliant customer support; affordable; multi-language options.

You can find a comprehensive comparison of survey platforms on Trust Radius.[7]

---

[6] T. Halford and C. McDonald, 'Are men taking up shared parental leave?' in *More or Less* for BBC Radio 4 (April 2016).

[7] Trust Radius. Available from: www.trustradius.com/surveys#overview

Please don't get blinded by design when choosing a survey platform. It's aesthetically tempting to build surveys that are easy on the eye, but the most important thing will always be WHY you are doing it.

To sum up

When used intentionally, surveys can be a great way to understand customers, but they can also be a waste of everyone's time. After reading this chapter, I don't want any of you to send out a survey for the sake of it. Create a survey because you want to find something out and because it's the right method for the job. Another useful (and cheap) way to understand customers is doing desk research or what we'll call secondary research. These days you won't need to spend hours in the library. You can simply use the internet.

Chapter 7 recap:

- Have a survey goal (what do I need to find out?).

- Human to human, not robot to human questions please.

- Use vetted existing tools to determine sample sizes.

- Test language and typos.

- Be transparent with your audience (why are you doing it? What are you going to do next?).

- Sweeten the deal if necessary.

- Use surveys for action (decisions, changes, improvements, more research).

- Surveys complement customer interviews; they don't replace them.

8 Learn about customers in your pyjamas and how to win at desk research

Free customer understanding, it's everywhere.
Whatever your business, chances are someone,
somewhere, has created something useful. Done
all the leg work, the recruiting, the interviews, the
surveys, the number crunching, the analysis and the
handy write-up.

What do we get? Market trends. Consumer habits.
Survey summaries. For free.

These insight goodies help you make better decisions,
reduce risk and give you fresh perspectives. They
make you feel less alone. All our businesses are
connected to stronger currents.

But you need to make it happen. The searching. The
reading. I can't do that for you (unless you pay me).
Whatever size your business, however niche you may
be, there will be something useful for you somewhere
on the internet.

Extract from Jungle Juice, 10th October 2022

D esk research is a form of secondary research that involves piggybacking off someone else's work. Easy. Nowadays, secondary research is painless. The internet gives us access to (nearly) everything. It won't ever replace primary research (getting out there and talking to our customers in real life) but it can be a quick and easy way to keep our finger on the pulse. In this chapter, I'll give you my best sources and tips for finding out useful stuff online. The best part? You can do it when you can't muster up the energy for any real customer interactions and can't be bothered to even get dressed.

What is desk research?

Everyone is pumping out research. From trade and industry associations, governments, consultancies to big tech giants and niche research agencies; there's a wealth of information out there waiting to be found. Most of it is high quality and rigorous, but always make sure you check the source and discard anything that reads fake. Misinformation is on the rise. Regularly looking up stuff about your business area can help you understand national and global trends and economic context. It provides you with customer behaviour and sentiment information you couldn't easily (and cheaply) identify yourself. It sparks innovation and brand-new thinking about your business. It can inspire you to try new things. Most of the time, secondary research costs little to nothing. Researchers at NN/g describe secondary research as standing on the shoulders of giants, not needing to reinvent the wheel every time.[1]

All businesses are connected to stronger currents. The economy, consumer morale, wars in foreign lands, these can all have an impact on your small business. First and foremost,

---

[1] M. Azarova, *Secondary Research*, Nielsen Norman Group (NN/g) (February 2022). Available from: www.nngroup.com/articles/secondary-research-in-ux

tapping into trend and market research reports gives you context. But it also gives you scale, as most of these studies have drawn on larger sample sizes over longer time periods. Desk research is also a great starting point for new product or service ideas, and a solid springboard for further bespoke customer investigation (surveys and customer interviews).

Where to look?

Most of your desk research will happen online, although if you fancy a day out in the real world some libraries have great business resource sections (if you are in London, the British Library has shelves of good stuff). Google (or your search engine of choice) is your starting point. In the search box, type your business area + consumer + trends. Easy-peasy. Let's take a few examples.

You make hand poured soy wax candles.
Type: candles + consumer + trends

You create content strategies for start-ups.
Type: start-up + content + trends

You make organic cotton sweatshirts for women.
Type: women + clothes + sustainable + insights

You are a personal trainer for teenagers.
Type: teenager + fitness + attitudes

The great thing with internet searches is there's no right or wrong. Try different combinations of words and terms, hit enter and see what comes back. Switch out some terms with others. Here are some useful keywords that, when combined with your area of business, generate results:

- Customer, consumer, client, community
- Parents, Gen Z, Baby Boomers, refugees

- London, European, Global, US, India
- Behaviour, sentiment, demand, trends
- Market, industry, sector
- Report, insight, analysis, forecast, research, survey

That's the proactive searching. Next up, some of my favourite go-to places to find easy-to-read and insightful reports (links to these can be found in the useful links section at the end of this book).

- **Think with Google.** Great for marketing research and digital trends. Innovative range of formats. Always something interesting to read.
- **Google Scholar.** Great for finding academic research on topics. You'll be surprised how many academics are researching day-to-day consumer trends and behaviours in different sectors.
- **Statistica.** Visualization of data across a range of areas alongside reports. The free version provides a wealth of interesting insights.
- **Hub Spot.** Marketing and social media business and consumer trends. Relevant for every type of business marketing itself online.
- **Enterprise Nation.** Online small business community. Picks up on relevant consumer trends and commissions its own research. Free to join.
- **Federation of Small Businesses.** Aimed at SMEs, its site has a free content hub with regular news and insight updates.
- **Ipsos.** A global leader in market research, Ipsos regularly publishes meaty, trusted reports on anything from consumer sentiment to how couples celebrate Valentine's Day.

- **Mintel**. A global market intelligence agency pumping out regular large-scale research reports. Their slogan: Experts in what consumers want and why.
- **Courier magazine**. This magazine for entrepreneurs has a comprehensive online resource library you can access for free. They also send out a brilliant newsletter.
- **Small Business**. Online news platform offering advice and ideas for small businesses and SMEs. They have a useful guides section with reports and research.
- **The UK Office for National Statistics (ONS)**. The place to go for any government-led research initiative. They have facts and figures for nearly all major business sectors. Don't let the word statistics put you off. It's more user-friendly than you might think.
- **Trade and industry bodies and associations**. Whether you're a florist, a baker, a marketer, a copywriter or an artist, chances are there's a trade association just for you. Go find yours.

Automate as much as you can when it comes to desk research. Sign up to newsletters from relevant sources to get new studies directly in your inbox. Not based in the UK? Fear not, most of these sources publish global trends and insights. For information on national trends relevant to your country and market, a few simple online searches will give you a list of sources you can draw upon.

Keeping one eye on the competition

In business, as much as possible, let's stay in our own lane. Spending too much time looking at competitors can be a distraction. But occasionally, it doesn't hurt to snoop. Especially when it comes to keeping tabs on what bigger brands are doing in your space. Desk research is perfect for that. What are they doing well? What ideas are they testing at scale? And what aren't they doing so well? Scan their website for latest offerings, pricing, testimonials and ratings. Dive into the comment sections on their social media pages and check what are people saying. Finally, read competitor reviews on sites such Google Reviews and Trustpilot. Our competitors shouldn't be our sole focus, after all how would they know what your customers want, but staying abreast of what others in your field are doing is good practice.

Get started

How do we fit desk research into our busy business lives? We make space. In my world, if it's not in the calendar, it won't happen. First, create a folder on your computer/email inbox called Market Research (or Customer Nuggets, Sparkly Unicorns or Mind-Blowing Stuff). That's where you'll squirrel away anything useful. But you need to come back to all these acorns. The following stretch task helps with that. Do now (or later).

Stretch task #5

- **Step 1**. Open calendar, diary or to-do list and add 30 minutes Market Research as an appointment with yourself on a set day.

- **Step 2**. When that set day comes, fire up your search engine of choice.

- **Step 3**. Type in your keyword(s) + customer + trend + report/insight and press enter (e.g. yoga retreat + Gen Z + customer trend report).

- **Step 4**. Scroll through first few pages of the search results (some gems to be found on page three, people!) and click on anything that takes your fancy.

- **Step 5**. Skim read headlines/report summary and save link or PDF to your newly created Market Research file.

- **Step 6**. Open calendar again and set another appointment for 30 minutes. Call it Read Market Research Stuff.

- **Step 7**. When said time comes, read what you found and make note of anything relevant.

- Do steps 1–5 a minimum of twice a year; go back to step 6 if you find anything new (see guidance on frequency for all appetites in Chapter 13).

To sum up

Desk research is easy, cheap as chips, and the perfect place to start if you're brand new to research. It won't replace speaking to your audience, but it can be a great source of quality, relevant insights that can be a starting point for your own research. In our next chapter, we'll stay on the topic of desk research. But instead of being on the hunt for trend reports, we'll explore another way of keeping tabs on customers, including (legally) listening in to online conversations, funky tools and AI, aka robots.

Chapter 8 recap:

- Desk research is a form of secondary research (using what is already there).

- Create a Market Research folder to store relevant insights.

- Compile a list of the most relevant sources for your business.

- Sign up to updates and newsletters to save time.

- Use Google (or your search engine of choice) for high-level searches.

- Desk research does not replace speaking to customers.

9 Can I pick my friend's nose? And how to be a digital spy

Can I pick my friend's nose?

The consensus is you can (pick your friend's nose) if you have their consent.

How do I know? Quora. For those of you who've been hiding under a rock for the last 10 years, Quora is a treasure trove for businesses.

It's full of randomness (yes there's a nose-picking thread) but the trained eye can feast on a well-categorized stream of unfiltered customer thoughts, opinions, questions and rants.

I bang on about talking to your customers, but social listening, well that's something you can do at home. Feet up. When you can't be bothered to speak to a soul.

Extract from Jungle Juice, 12th May 2022

If you have a bricks and mortar business, you can indulge in some real-life spying, people watching if you like. Small businesses learn lots by observing how people browse, choose and buy in the real world. In the digital world, you can do it too. But instead of watching people, you're watching their comments, discussions, threads and conversations. In this next chapter you'll discover the best hot spots for virtual eavesdropping, how to use tools such as AnswerThePublic and AlsoAsked and learn how you can use AI to your advantage.

Being a digital spy

Social listening is being a digital spy (it's perfectly legal by the way). These days, people share widely (and wildly) on the internet, and we can listen and observe. The cheapest front row seats ever. We can hear what people say they want and don't want. Keep track on what they're raving about and read the latest dirt they've dished on Trustpilot. All in their own words. With a little help from our AI robot friends, we can spot patterns and recurring themes that sharpen our understanding.

What you need to be a digital spy:

- A device connected to the internet.
- An idea of what you are looking for (crucial if you don't want to fall into a cat meme trap).
- A timer to limit the time spent on this activity (otherwise, well... see cat meme reason above).

Thanks to our growing human tendency to bare our souls online, combined with a flurry of grown-up platforms and tools to help us tap into what's being said, small businesses can learn so much more about customers. We just need to know where to look.

Where should you look?

Search *social-listening tools* and you'll be overwhelmed with results. Bigger brands use them to keep tabs on what people are saying about them, pre-empt PR disasters and get a handle on customer behaviour and sentiment. Chances are your brilliant businesses aren't generating the same volume of mentions online but that doesn't mean you shouldn't listen. You want to be listening to online customer conversations and comments *within* your business area. Understanding what is delighting and pissing people off in your space.

Here are some good starting points. You'll need to set up an account to use some of these platforms, a minor inconvenience for the treasure trove of conversations you'll get in return.

- **Quora**. A global online platform where users can ask questions and get answers on just about any topic under the sun. Content and Q&As are organized in spaces (e.g. photography, fitness, entrepreneurship, etc.). Quora has lofty ambitions: 'We want to connect the people who have knowledge to the people who need it, to bring together people with different perspectives so they can understand each other better.' Requires an account (free).
- **Reddit**. A social news aggregation, content rating and discussion website. With 52 million daily active users users and over 130k communities, Reddit is a window into what is trending now, what people are talking about and reading. Requires an account (free).
- **Amazon reviews**. For product businesses, search for similar products and check out the reviews. If you are a service business, look at business books in your business sector. Pay specific attention to the one-to-two-star reviews. That's where you'll find ideas about how you could evolve your offer.
- **Call-in radio shows**. Old-school and brilliant for listening to people explain their points of view in their own words. Personal favourite for juicy insights: *You and Yours* (BBC Radio 4) and the *Jeremy Vine show*

(BBC Radio 2). For these shows you can search the archive online to select topics relevant to your business.

- **Review sites.** Google reviews, Trustpilot and Yelp are a treasure trove of customer satisfaction and dissatisfaction – check out what folks are raving about or screaming about in your business area.
- **Social media.** Accounts in your business area with big followings are a good place to start as they tend to get hundreds of comments. Tapping into smaller and fully engaged audiences works well too.

Checking these types of platforms can be quite a manual process but it's more than worth it (and not just for the memes) on a regular basis.

Search listening tools

With 8.5 billion searches typed into Google daily (that's 90k every second), tapping into search engine data is another way of getting under the skin of your customers. If you knew what your customer was searching, how useful would that be? How could it help us understand better what they need? What they're struggling with? What content to create? What language do they use? What new offers to build?

Introducing AnswerThePublic and AlsoAsked. Two useful tools that help you do just that. Powered by actual Google search data, these two platforms are a direct line into your customers' minds. Free (within reason), they do all the heavy lifting for you. You type in your relevant keywords and within seconds you're shown what people have been searching for on or around that topic. While both rely on Google, the type of data they use is different.

AnswerThePublic uses Google autocomplete data. Let's be honest, these days we rarely type in more than a couple of words in Google's search box. As soon as we start typing,

Google appears to read our mind and makes a list of handy suggestions we click on instead. In search terms, this list of suggestions is called autocomplete data. And it's not Google making up the suggestions. Autocomplete data stems from real (and full) searches people still make daily.

AlsoAsked aggregates data from the *People Also Ask* section on the Google search results page (have a look next time you do a Google search, and you'll see it two-thirds down the page). Essentially, it gives you an idea of all the other relevant and connected questions people are searching around your selected keywords.

I suggest using AnswerThePublic in the first instance to get a broad overview of what people are searching for around your keywords. For example, if you type in *business market research* in AnswerThePublic, you will get results organized under headings such as *Why, Can, Where, When, Will, Are*, etc. Under each heading there will be a list of questions such as *Why do businesses conduct market research? How do businesses use market research? Where to find business market research?* You get the gist.

AlsoAsked is best for drilling down into a specific search query and looking at all connected questions. Let's take our *business market research* example again. The results for this search are split into four related questions (remember, based on the *People Also Ask* data):

- What is business market research?
- What are the four types of market research?
- What is a market research business example?
- What type of business is market research?

Each of these questions is split out further into more specific questions. For instance, under *What is business market research?* I found:

- What is called business research?
- What is [a] business research process?

- Why do business market research?
- What is the concept of the research? etc.

Results from both platforms are visual, useful and can be downloaded in different formats. While both restrict the number of free searches, you get more than enough chances to find out something valuable. Here are some common use cases for businesses:

- Content creation (the questions people are asking that you could answer with your content)
- Product and service ideas (what are people regularly struggling with? Where are the opportunities?)
- Search Engine Optimization (SEO) (what keywords do I need to include on my website to be found by the right audience?)
- Google Ads – popular keywords for ad strategies
- Marketing copy (how can I speak my customers' language? What terms are my customers using?)

There are other smaller players leveraging the power of computers to help understand customer behaviour. Tori Rosevink is Chief Insight Officer at Categoracle, a start-up in the food and drinks space. Online food and drink reviews are insight rich. Thousands of punters give their opinions on anything from keto crisps to the latest alcohol-free beer brand. If you want to make any sense of them, you might as well block out your calendar for the next six months. Manually it would take at least that long, if not longer. Categoracle uses text analytics technology to crawl through thousands of Trustpilot reviews for different food and drink categories and squeezes out all the useful stuff into off-the-shelf reports.

Tori has seen many a small business get excited about their new mushroom crisps, or herb infused seltzer, but founder excitement doesn't always lead to product success. Tori told me:

Doing research before you spend a penny on your business is just so worthwhile and valuable. If you think about it, it's the cheapest moment to tweak your idea. And when I say cheapest, I mean both financially and emotionally.

Scared of robots?

New tools to help businesses process and understand large customer data sets emerge all the time. The latest crop is powered by AI. In her article 'What is AI?' Aruna Pattam explains that AI involves using computers to do things that traditionally required human intelligence:

> AI can process large amounts of data in ways that humans cannot. The goal for AI is to be able to do things like recognize patterns, make decisions and judge like humans. To do this, we need lots of data inputted into them.[1]

ChatGPT is a prime example. This AI-powered chat bot attracted over a million users in its first five days. It's an artificial brain that speaks (think types) like a human. You can converse with it (online) and ask it questions. You can even ask it to write a blog post for your website about the benefits of buying candles (I know because I asked). It's not connected to the internet and as of writing this book hasn't got a clue about events post 2021. ChatGPT has learnt everything it knows from humans and has been fed vast amounts of data written by humans.

---

[1] A. Pattam, *Artificial Intelligence, in simple terms*, LinkedIn (June 2021). Available from: www.linkedin.com/pulse/artificial-intelligence-simple-terms-aruna-pattam/?trk=public_profile_article_view

Use cases for smaller businesses are still emerging, from support with content creation (think the bones of your post) to the ability to process vast amounts of qualitative data (think reviews, testimonials, interview transcripts) and derive sentiment and meaning (sensemaking, see how to do it without robots back in Chapter 6). One thing's for sure, these technological advances level the playing field with bigger brands, many of which have been beavering away for years developing their own AI tools.

Embrace the tools, give them a try. You've nothing to lose. As Tori told me:

> They're fantastic at doing the heavy lifting and they will get you a long way. And each iteration of these tools gets you that little bit closer to a machine doing it for you. But it's never going to be the same as an actual human. You will always need the human for art and creativity.

To sum up

As this chapter has shown, there are loads of ways to *spy* on customers online. Not in a creepy, unethical way but by tapping into conversations and behaviours taking place in the digital universe. Digital spying can take on many forms: reading scathing reviews from disgruntled customers, eavesdropping on chat forums or listening to people share their views on the radio. I also shared some useful online tools to use that do the leg work for you (e.g. AnswerThePublic and AlsoAsked). And then there is AI. While in desperate need of regulation (at the point of publication this had yet to happen), AI *can* be a useful recourse for budget-tight and time-poor businesses. Let's down tools for our next chapter and explore another way of understanding what your customers think. Feedback.

Chapter 9 recap:

- Look for where customers hang out online and listen in on conversations.

- Use sites such as Reddit, Quora, Amazon.

- Leverage Google search data through platforms like AnswerThePublic or AlsoAsked.

- Explore the opportunities AI can bring to your business.

- Don't be (too) scared of robots.

10 Stop asking for five-star feedback

Feedback lifts you, feedback triggers. We want it…
but preferably five stars. If we're not careful, feedback
meddles with self-worth. Defensiveness rears its ugly
head.

As a customer, giving honest feedback is tough too,
right? Especially to our small business pals. The good
news. We CAN get better at asking, receiving and
giving feedback.

Extract from Jungle Juice, 1st November 2021

Feedback is another way to understand how customers feel
about our business. It can be a springboard for improvement
and innovation. It can comfort us (all the hard
work has been worth it). When negative, it can crush us and
rile us. In this chapter, we'll look at why you need feedback
(and not just the good stuff), how to ask for it and how to take
it like a champ.

What is customer feedback?

Feedback is 'advice, criticism or information about how good or useful something or somebody's work is.'[1] In big companies, feedback is often woven into the customer experience. Feedback requests are automated and pop up when you're browsing. You get emails after a purchase. In shops, screens ask for emoji feedback. On the phone to a company? You're asked to take part in a feedback survey before you can get anywhere near a human.

As with surveys, customer feedback fatigue is real. It's not so much the request for feedback that's grating consumers these days but more the fact that companies are doing nothing with it. Sixty-seven per cent of customers said brands need to get better at listening to feedback.[2] For customers, listening is caring. For smaller business, asking for feedback tends to be more ad hoc. We either apologize for asking (very British trait), ask when we know it'll be good (nothing wrong with that), or we word (subconsciously no doubt) our requests in such a way our customers think twice about telling us what they really think. Other times, we ask, but do nothing with the feedback and then, well, some of us don't ask at all.

But feedback is important. We learn from it and hear customers in their own words. We find patterns and make changes for the better. We need to get used to it however uncomfortable it may feel. Let's normalize asking and receiving feedback, and where relevant, choosing to do something with it. Let feedback fatigue be an opportunity for smaller business to do what bigger brands aren't visibly doing enough

---

[1] Oxford Learners Dictionaries' definition. Available from: www.oxfordlearnersdictionaries.com/definition/english/feedback?q=feedback

[2] L. Brown, M. Dorsey and B. Temkin, *What your customers need you to know for the year ahead*, Qualtrics. Available from: www.qualtrics.com/uk/ebooks-guides/uk-consumer-trends-report-2022

of: listening, showing they care, responding (with grace) and where appropriate, taking action.

Feedback formats

Feedback comes in many guises and can be directly solicited (e.g. feedback surveys, ratings, reviews, and testimonials, for example) but also unsolicited. These days any disgruntled customer can make their opinion known. There's very little you can do about it. For smaller businesses, one bad review can sting and hurt your business. Making it clear that you are open to feedback at every stage of the customer journey avoids unsolicited scathing reviews. Gripes can be nipped in the bud before they hit the public realm.

At the heart of feedback is the idea we don't have all the answers. That there's space for improvement, that we're confident enough to listen to other people's opinions and astute enough to know what feedback to keep and what to discard.

New York Times bestselling author and speaker Diana Kander told me:

> You know you're not being curious enough when it comes to customer feedback, the more comfortable you feel. If you're getting 90% of thumbs up when you ask for feedback, or even worse, you assume that no news is good news, you might be missing something. If you believe that when something isn't working your customers will tell you about it... you're wrong. We're all nice people and we don't want to hurt people's feelings. We'll just quietly take our business elsewhere.

How to ask for it

Anyone can ask for feedback but asking for *useful* feedback requires bravery. It can be exposing, and our egos don't like it. As a result, we rarely get to the customer truth. People sense whether you can handle hearing what they really think and adjust their feedback accordingly. In a Tweet, author and organizational psychologist Adam Grant says: 'When people don't hesitate to give you feedback, it's a sign of trust. They have faith that you'll take it as an opportunity to grow and not as a threat to your ego.'[3]

Let's start with how NOT to ask for it. I like my gym. It's cheap, local and well equipped. But the way they ask for feedback is all wrong. Everywhere you look there are five-star feedback requests (no doubt linked to staff perks). Not a simple give us feedback or a tell us what you think but give us FIVE-star feedback. Asking systematically for five stars won't get you far. How can we improve if we only ever ask for the good stuff?

In some spaces, such as the podcast world, anything but a five-star review just doesn't cut the mustard (judging by the number of times podcast hosts say it). The system seems to be set up to reward perfection from the get-go, with only five-star podcasts suggested to listeners. I disagree with this approach. If you operate in one of those only-five-stars-will-do digital spaces, make sure to seek out honest views by other means.

So how do we ask? How do we make our customers feel safe enough to tell us what they really think? This is especially important in smaller sized businesses, as the relationship between you and your customer is often more intimate.

Try the following tips for size. Subtle changes in the way we ask for feedback can help our customers feel comfortable telling us what they really think. That's what we want, isn't it?

- **Ask for advice, not for feedback**. Thanks so much for attending my workshop, I'd love to get your advice on

---

[3] A. Grant, Twitter (October 2023). Available from: https://twitter.com/AdamMGrant/status/1451957447019663360

how I could improve the next one – this request gives space to hear all your customer's thoughts.

- **Put them in your shoes**. I'm thinking of making a few changes to my online shop. I know you are a loyal customer. If this was your online shop, what would you change?
- **Be specific**. Nothing like constraints to focus the mind. What three things would you change if this was your product? What are the three things you enjoyed/ struggled with the most?
- **Reward honesty**. If you want to continue to get honest feedback, show the giver what you did with it. Thank them. It will encourage them to be honest again next time.

These suggestions work in real-life situations and online. But do yourself a huge favour, when seeking out more honest feedback, only ask (read or look) when you're ready to receive.

How to take it

In a world that thrives on positive feedback, it's exposing, embarrassing and excruciating to get anything but. *Likes* are our digital currency. And so often as small businesses, what we sell and who we are become one.

Sara Fortier from Outwitly shared her experience of getting negative feedback and how hard it can be to shake off:

If you get a piece of feedback on your business you take it personally because your business is you. Work towards mentally separating the two. You are not your company, and you are worthy regardless of the success of your business. But, if you're not careful, you start avoiding seeking out feedback because you don't want to deal with the heartbreak.

Sara is right, it's hard. Science shows us why. Any feedback perceived as negative sends our brains into a panic. Literally. In her TED talk, *The Secret to Giving Great Feedback*,[4] cognitive scientist LeeAnne Renninger explains how the part of our brains called the amygdala is constantly scanning our environment for information perceived as a social threat. How do we override this neurological wiring? First and foremost, with awareness and practice.

When I first started sending out my newsletter, Jungle Juice, I took unsubscribes personally. When I recognized an email address, it was worse. I know I'm not alone. One business owner told me she used to send a follow-up email to every person who unsubscribed asking them what she had done wrong. People have so many reasons for not wanting your stuff anymore: inbox overwhelm, bad hair day, sickness or your content triggers them in some way (that's on them not you). If you have a mass exodus, then yes, seeking answers is sensible but if you have an overwhelmingly happy community and are only saying bye to a few folks along the way, then leave that scab alone.

I'm much better at leaning into feedback these days. Even if it's something my brain (and ego) dislikes. After a live workshop I ran, one participant politely said I hadn't managed the attendees' speaking time adequately (some people don't half love to talk). I followed up straight away thanking her for her feedback. I said she had a valid point and that managing participants' airtime in workshops was something I was activity working on. She was grateful for the follow-up.

If practice makes things easier, setting yourself up for success is my second piece of advice. Only ask for the real stuff if you are mentally ready to receive it. Had a crap day? Reading comments from someone telling you how to improve your website might

---

[4] L. Renninger, *The secret to giving feedback*, TED (February 2020). Available from: www.ted.com/talks/leeann_renninger_the_secret_ to_giving_great_feedback/transcript

not be the best remedy to lift those spirits. Confidence a bit low? Rummaging through the one-star reviews on your latest product launch is not the best use of your time. Delve into feedback when you are mentally ready to receive.

Diana Kander is a big fan of asking customers for feedback. She recommends starting with the good stuff as positive blind spots also get missed.

> Talk to your satisfied customers and ask them what it is that they love about your product and service and how they explain it to others. I bet you'll hear some surprising feedback about things you do that really matter to them. What you'll also realize is things you think are important, that take up a lot of time, aren't as valuable to customers as you thought.

Let's take Diana's advice and start with the positive. As small businesses we need to learn to take the good, the bad and the ugly. Without getting defensive. It's hard, but we can get better at it.

How to use it

American professor, lecturer, author and podcast host Brené Brown's mantra for feedback is: 'Be brave. Listen. You can take what's helpful and leave the rest.'[5] We are not at our customers' total mercy. We can disagree with feedback. How *do* we figure out when feedback is useful? When feedback stings, there is often some truth in it. The key is to ride out the initial emotion of being under attack and the defensive rhetoric that follows (how dare they! I gave that my all. They were shitty customers anyway). When you receive something that stings tell yourself:

---

[5] B. Brown, Twitter (July 2019). Available from: https://twitter.com/BreneBrown/status/1148718360496136192

- I am not under threat. I am safe.
- There will be no humiliation on the public square involving a pillory.
- I can take the time I need to digest before responding.
- I can take what I need and leave the rest.

Stay honest with yourself, allow yourself to be vulnerable (yes, it's uncomfortable) and give yourself the space to process feedback. And then action only what will strengthen your business.

Testimonials and reviews

It's worth spending a few lines on testimonials and reviews, two common forms of feedback. A testimonial is a *controlled* way of getting feedback. We ask a customer or client to showcase the best of their experience doing business with us. We upload testimonials to our websites and social media channels. They are effective at showing the client transformation and the impact your offer brings. And they're almost always positive. We often forget to ask for testimonials from our happiest customers so let this be a reminder. Ideally, you can help your customer structure theirs by offering a few prompts (three questions to answer can be a good place to start). Don't be afraid to ask and make a request promptly after the product or service has been delivered, while it's fresh in their mind.

Reviews are not as easily controlled, as social proof agency Boast explains:

> Customers have final say in where they post reviews, but you can encourage them to leave reviews in the best possible places. The best place for your happy

customer to leave reviews is where the maximum number of customers will see your business.[6]

Reviews are hugely important in driving customer behaviour. In the article 'Online reviews: statistics that will blow your mind,' Finnish digital trust firm Trustmary says 93% of customers read reviews before making a purchase and 58% of consumers would be ready to pay more or travel further afield to visit companies with good reviews.[7]

While customers can drop a review (good or bad) on a third-party site whether you want them to or not, increase the chances of getting positive reviews by asking satisfied customers for them on a regular basis. Customers rarely wake up thinking, *Right, I'm going to write a review today.* You need to prompt them, nudge them in the gentlest possible way. But do ask.

How to give it

Why not learn to give better feedback too? Thus, creating a virtuous small business feedback loop of sorts. I believe we can up our game when giving feedback to other small businesses. Giving honest feedback sometimes puts us in a vulnerable position so here are a few suggestions:

- If you have negative feedback, start by contacting them directly (as opposed to writing a negative review online) – always give people the benefit of the doubt.

---

[6] S. Stemler, *Testimonials vs reviews: what's the difference and why does it matter?*, Boast (November 2022). Available from: https://boast.io/testimonial-vs-review-whats-the-difference-and-why-does-it-matter

[7] Trustmary, *Online reviews: statistics that will blow your mind* [2023], trustmary.com (March 2023). Available from: https://trustmary.com/reviews/online-reviews-statistics-that-will-blow-your-mind

- Be sensitive about how and when you give your feedback (think words you use and timing). Not everyone is ready to receive.
- Sometimes it just won't be worth it. Feedback isn't always a gift well received.

To sum up

They say feedback is a gift, but the reality is often so different and difficult. This chapter shows how feedback can be a springboard for improvement and innovation in your business but only if you know how to ask for it and receive it. No more hunting down five-star reviews only (however brilliant they make us feel). Lean into all of it. The good, the bad and don't-waste-too-much-time-on the ugly. Take what is useful (and be honest about that part) and screw the rest. Next up, something we can control more intentionally than customer feedback. Roll up your sleeves, let's get testing.

> ### Chapter 10 recap:
>
> - Feedback comes in many guises (surveys, ratings, reviews, testimonials, direct etc.).
>
> - Feedback is always an opportunity to learn.
>
> - To get useful feedback frame it as a request for advice.
>
> - Be specific (e.g. what three things would you change?).
>
> - Reward honesty (you'll increase your chances of getting truthful feedback next time around).
>
> - Make sure you're in the right frame of mind before asking for feedback.

- You are not your business so try not to take negative feedback personally.

- Be sensitive, considerate and realistic when it comes to giving feedback to other businesses.

11 Small business testing

Nobody bought me coffee and that's ok. A few months ago, I added a link to Ko-fi at the bottom of my newsletter. I magpied the idea from other newsletters with bigger audiences.

Let's give that a try, I told myself. It felt cheeky (Brits asking for coffee money) and impulsive.

I didn't ask my community beforehand, and I didn't extensively research the monetization of email. I just opened Ko-fi, created a profile, whipped up a few words and stuck a link at the bottom of Jungle Juice.

And nobody bought me a coffee.

What does that tell me? Nobody likes my newsletter? Unlikely. Plenty of opens, week after week. Subscribers thought maybe next time? Or maybe, just maybe, tipping a business content creator is not your thing. My point? It was a low-risk test, quick and free. And it told me what I needed to know for now.

So, I'll continue to buy my own coffee for a while and that's fine too.

Extract from Jungle Juice, 17th October 2022

Testing ideas doesn't have to be cumbersome. Testing doesn't have to follow a complicated process. Sometimes doing IS the testing and the results help you decide where to focus your time and when you might be onto something, or not. In this next chapter, we'll explore how to test your ideas. Testing is, after all, another market research method. I'll also share THE most important question to ask yourself before you create anything new. And finally, we'll look at price. We'll hear from an experienced pricing expert and solve some of your most pressing price conundrums when it comes to testing price with customers.

Quick and dirty testing

There's lots of advice online on how to test ideas but as a small business be mindful of efforts versus rewards. With limited time and resource, we're aiming for quick and dirty testing not full-scale lab-style testing. Sometimes *doing* is the research and when you start your experiments early, so little is at stake, so go for it. Innovation consultancy Strategyzer has some solid advice: 'Consider cost, data reliability and time required when you design a mix of experiments. As a rule of thumb, start cheap when uncertainty is high and increase your spending on experiments with increasing certainty.'[1]

Let's kick-off this chapter with some practical ways to test business ideas. If your idea is more complex or requires software development, include meatier testing. Strategyzer wrote a great book *Testing Business Ideas* that'll help you with just that.

- **The waitlist.** A simple way of testing demand without a finished product. A waitlist is essentially a list of names and email addresses people have willingly given you after

---

[1] A. Osterwalder, Y. Pigneur, G. Bernarda and A. Smith, *Value Proposition Design*, John Wiley & Sons, p. 216 (2014).

reading about your future product. This method relies on you marketing your idea. You can't just promote it once and take poor sign-ups as an indicator that your idea is doomed. Give it a chance by actively talking about it over several weeks. Set yourself a target beforehand. How many names on the waitlist would mean success to you?

- **Ad testing**. If you know your way around Google and Facebook Ads, creating mock promotions for your business idea is another way to test a concept. For small businesses with smaller audiences, ads can be an effective way to increase your reach (it'll cost you though). They can be tricky to set up if you've never done it before, so I would always recommend getting some pro help. Positive interest could equate to someone clicking on a 'learn more' button, for example.
- **Mock sales**. There's nothing like someone whipping out their bank card to show real intent. The mock sales page test is one step further than the waitlist. You create a sales page on your website with a clear description of the product or service you're testing (but haven't created yet). You add a 'buy now' button. Some business experiment specialists go so far as to collect bank card details on a dummy form to simulate a real purchase. This comes with some caveats but can be super-powerful for gauging willingness to pay. Strategyzer recommends notifying the customer straight after they've completed a mock purchase. Be transparent about what information you'll keep and what you'll erase. Offer a reward for participating in the test. 'Don't fear mock sales will alienate customers and negatively affect your brand. Manage customer perceptions well and mock sales can be turned into an advantage,' Strategyzer says.[2]

---

[2] A. Osterwalder, Y. Pigneur, G. Bernarda and A. Smith, *Value Proposition Design*, John Wiley & Sons, p. 237 (2014).

- **Split testing (or A/B testing).** This involves presenting your audience with two different variants of the same thing. It could be two versions of an advert (see ad testing above) or two content types (static images versus video). It could also be two versions of a webpage on your website, a sign-up form or a button placement. It could even be as small as a subject line on your newsletter. You send each version to distinct audiences to see which ones get more traction. Testing with smaller audiences can be a challenge. There are plenty of off-the-shelf tools that support split testing, just make sure you have the traffic numbers to back up a decision. Thirty people coming to your website over two weeks – 17 of which clicked on version 1 and 13 of which clicked on version 2 – is less clear-cut than doing the experiment with 3,000 site visits over the same period.

- **Buy a feature.** This test works well when you already have an idea with legs. You've validated the concept and checked there's a need. Now you're trying to decide how to start. Imagine you're launching a new backpack for hybrid workers. You're trying to decide what the first prototype will look like. You have options: buttons or zips; water bottle holder or not; waterproof bag cover or not. As well as colour and internal pocket options. You start by making a list of all the features you aspire to have and invite people from your target audience to play. You price each of your features according to how much effort/cost they'll take you to implement. You make sure all the features add up to MORE than £100. You give each person a fictional £100 and then ask them which features they would buy. As they can't buy all the features, it forces them to think about what matters to them. You can do this with service base businesses too. If you are testing a new three-week programme for coaches, you could list all the things you *could* do (video recordings after sessions, transcript of sessions, workbooks, FB groups, etc.) and see what really matters to your audience.

- **Newsletter.** This one is more of a slow burner but if you have a newsletter, it's a great virtual space to test things out. Content, concepts, workshops and new product ideas. It's a direct line into a captive and friendly audience.
- **IRL testing.** This requires a little more in-real-life (IRL) energy to pull off. It could be as small as having a stall at a well-attended local market with a small sample of your products or as involved as organizing a free session at your co-working space or local community centre.

Whatever test you use, always include a Call to Action (CTA). A CTA is an action the customer must do and requires some effort. This could be clicking a button, typing in an email address, answering a survey or entering in bank card information. 'The more the customer (test subject) has to invest to perform a CTA, the stronger the evidence that he or she is really interested,' explains Strategyzer.[3]

Creating a minimum viable product (MVP) is another way of testing an idea with your audience. Don't let the start-up lingo put your off, an MVP is essentially the smallest thing (think cheapest and easiest) you can create that still adds value to your audience. Pretty straightforward, let's dive in.

What's your skateboard?

Henrick Kniberg's skateboard sketch (see Figure 1) is a viral legend in the innovation space. While both step-by-step

---

[3] A. Osterwalder, Y. Pigneur, G. Bernarda and A. Smith, *Value Proposition Design*, John Wiley & Sons, p. 218 (2014).

sketches end with a car, Henrick, an author, and agile and lean consultant at Crisp, shows us two very different ways of getting there. The first makes the customer wait and wait and wait until the car is ready (and we finally get a smile). The second gives the customer something usable every step of the way. In every product iteration, there is value. You won't get to London on a skateboard fast, but you will get somewhere.

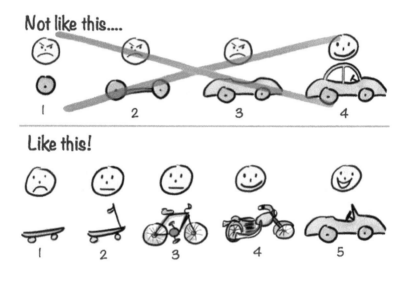

Figure 1: Minimum viable product by Henrik Kniberg[4]

The skateboard sketch is of course a metaphor, not a depiction of real car development. That's missing the point. This sketch is about iterative design. An invitation not to build the perfect, end-goal product or service in one go. Many products

---

[4] H. Kniberg, *Not like this, like this and Minimum Viable Product,* blog.crisp.se (January 2016). Available from: https://blog.crisp.se/2016/01/25/henrikkniberg/making-sense-of-mvp, reproduced here under Creative Commons https://www.crisp.se/konsulter/henrik-kniberg/faq

have died a slow painful death because businesses spent too much time building behind closed doors, waiting for it all to be perfect. Come launch day, they realize customers have simply moved on.

With iterative design, we release and learn. Every lesson is fed back into the next iteration. But each version must stand on its own two feet. People don't want half a car; they want a skateboard. Here are a few examples in Table 5.

Table 5: Examples of MVP for different business types

Business type	First iteration	Second iteration	Third iteration	End goal
Email marketing services	Free newsletter with marketing tips	Free 30 minutes masterclass on how to write good email subject lines	Paid 90 minutes workshop	Three-week online email marketing course
Fitness instructor	Share fitness tips on social media	Online live fitness class (small groups)	Paid IRL group fitness classes	1:1 personal training session
Food and drink	Tea and cakes party	Farmer's market stall	Pop-up café	Open a café

So, by all means, think big, but start small. Now, let's tackle price. Testing price with customers is tricky. Let me help.

Testing price

Struggling with pricing? You're not alone. Big businesses struggle too. Testing willingness to pay (WTP) is not asking your customers *How much would you pay for this?* In his book

Running Lean, Ash Maurya writes: 'There is no reasonable economic justification for a customer to offer anything but a low-ball figure.'[5] Makes sense. He adds: 'Usually the right price is one the customer accepts, but with a little resistance.'[6]

I once tested price for a small business client. The offer was a monthly subscription fee to access a private group of local independent businesses. Think online membership, useful resources and access to business-related webinars and events. The starting price, I thought, was too low for the work potentially involved in building this offer. But we rolled with it and tested it. And it was indeed too low. Every person we spoke to said yes without the slightest hesitation. *No* resistance whatsoever. Beware of the easy yes.

When testing price with customers, head into your interview with a range, something the customer can react to. How do we set that initial price range? Tamara Milacic runs price consultancy Nine Nine Lab. She advises small business to take both an internal and external lens when coming up with that initial pricing range. The internal lens stems from knowing your numbers. 'You need to ask yourself: how do I make sure my product or service is profitable? What does this cost me to make or create? What are my margins?' she says.

Next, the external lens, when we look outside our business and validate our pricing in the market. Find two or three competitors (comparable offer and target market) and check their prices. Tammara told me:

> Two to three, absolute maximum. Beyond that it's analysis paralysis. Looking at those competitors and factoring in your internal price information will give you your price range... It's then up to you to decide how you're going to pitch yourself. As a price leader

[5] A. Maurya, *Running Lean* (2nd edition), O'Reilly, p. 98 (2012).
[6] A. Maurya, *Running Lean* (2nd edition), O'Reilly, p. 106 (2012).

(cheaper end of the scale), as a mid-market offer or premium (higher end).

Value-based pricing is seen by many pricing experts as the final pricing frontier. Popular among experienced service providers, value-based price offers are established on how valuable they are to customers. The same product could be priced differently for two different clients, based on the value they place on it. This does imply knowing (or finding out) what value our customers place on our offer in the first place. This route can get muddy for small businesses and is far from an exact science. But there are some clever tools and methods out there that can help both product and service businesses tap into value-based selling.

Gabor-Granger and Van Westendorp are two survey-based price research methods that aren't half as complicated as they sound (both named after British and Dutch economists, respectively). They help businesses test WTP and assess the optimum value (and price) customers place on a product or service. Both pricing survey methods consist of asking respondents a series of simple questions.

The Gabor-Granger survey asks respondents to say whether they'd pay for your offer at a set price. For example: Would you pay £50 for this? Yes/no. If the respondent says yes then it will move up a price level. Next question would be: Would you pay £60 for this? Yes/no, etc. At scale, and with the relevant audience, you get to an optimum price. Use the Gabor-Granger method for testing price increases on existing products, new pricing for an improved (existing) product and/or testing price for offers under £25.

The Van Westendorp method, on the other hand, extracts price sensitivity and the relationship between customer perception of quality and price. It's best used for higher-value items, as well as brand-new products and services. It uses four questions to determine an optimum price:

1. At what price would this product be so expensive you wouldn't consider it?
2. At what price would this product be so cheap you'd feel the quality is poor?
3. At what price would this product start to get expensive enough that you'd still consider buying it, but you'd have to give it some thought?
4. At what price would you feel this product is a bargain and great value for money?

You can find both methodologies online and set up your own survey, but if you are going to do it alone, a couple of things to watch out for:

- **Sample size.** For this to be effective you need to have a decent online sample size (100+ people). If you don't have that kind of audience, consider using a third party who can set the survey up for you and access a wider, targeted audience to ensure the statistical relevance.
- **Offer.** For both methods, you need to accurately describe and position the offer you are testing.
- **Price points.** You need to have a price range in mind before you set up your survey.

To sum up

Testing early and often reduces risks, builds confidence, step by step, iteration by iteration. Like a diligent dung beetle, meticulously rolling its pungent prize down a hill. Testing can be lightweight and remember that sometimes *doing* is the testing. Hopefully, this chapter also boosted your pricing confidence. Businesses need good pricing, and good pricing comes from being more intentional and taking full advantage of the tools at our disposal.

Next up: an oxymoron. A chapter about *not* listening to customers in a book about listening to customers. I wrote this chapter because you matter too. As a freelancer, a small business owner or founder don't lose yourself in the sometimes-confusing cacophony of customers. Our next chapter looks precisely at when you shouldn't listen to a word they say.

Chapter 11 recap:

- Use a range of methods (waitlist, mock sales, newsletter, A/B testing, etc.) to test ideas with customers.

- Always ask yourself what is the smallest thing (your skateboard) you can create that still adds value?

- Don't ask customers what they are willing to pay.

- Set a price range based on internal and external factors.

- Look for verbal and non-verbal cues when mentioning a price.

- Use pricing surveys where appropriate.

12 When not to listen to customers

Listen to customers. But filter. As businesses we could do ALL the things. However, successful businesses do a few things REALLY well. They launch something because it makes sense. They pivot because it makes sense. They grow because it makes sense. They deliberately stay small because it makes sense to THEM.

Listen to customers, absolutely, but don't lose yourself. We're all looking for that elusive sweet spot. You'll know when you're there: it lights a fire in your belly, delights your customers and pays those bills.

If it doesn't. Ignore, move on, and keep looking.

Extract from Jungle Juice, 30ᵗʰ May 2022

This chapter might come as a surprise. After all, *Do Penguins Eat Peaches?* is a book about *listening* to customers, not ignoring them. But there are situations when ignoring them is the right thing to do. It will require you to take a step back, to take a breath and think about whether what customers are asking for is what *you* really want. This penultimate chapter unpicks five reasons where you have full permission to say *no*!

Reason 1: The customer is not aligned with your business values

So much talk about values in business and in life. Lots of eye-rolling too (bit touchy-feely). But values help you make decisions and can act as a North Star. It might take a bit of time upfront to figure out yours (see stretch task #6 at the end of this section) but once you have them, decision making is easier. If customers request something that doesn't feel right, it probably means what they're requesting doesn't align with your values.

Let's say you sell make-up. You are getting frequent requests from customers to launch a young girls' make-up range. This is something you could technically do but it just doesn't sit well with you. Your values are *authenticity* and *wellbeing*. Even if you have mums of girls begging you to develop a girl-friendly range, this time you decide not to listen. When you're clear about your values, these types of decisions are easier to make.

I put off the *finding your values* exercise until I had to (building my brand kit). Backed into a corner, I turned to American professor, lecturer, author and podcast host Brené Brown. In her book *Daring Greatly*, she says:

> Living into our values means that we do more than profess our values, we practice them. We walk our talk – we are clear about what we believe and hold important, and we take care that our intentions, words, thoughts and behaviours align with those beliefs.[1]

Sounds easy in practice but it can take a bit of work to get there. Brené suggests having two values. It can take a few rounds of staring at a list of values (your starting point) to

---

[1] B. Brown, *Dare to lead list of values*, brenebrown.com. Available from: https://brenebrown.com/resources/dare-to-lead-list-of-values

narrow things down to two. My suggestion is not to get too hung up on how many you're left with and to edit them down gradually (FYI mine are curiosity and courage).

Remember, as you change, your business changes and your values will too. And that's ok. Lots of people attempt the values exercise and give up. It does require some brain power. But it's so worth it. Come back to this one fresh.

Stretch task #6

- Download a list of values (plenty to choose from online).

- Set your timer for 10 minutes.

- Read the values on your list and circle 10 that jump out at you (no overthinking!).

- Take a closer look at the 10 you've chosen and see if there is any overlap between some of them.

- Cut down to five.

- Rank the five you have left.

- Pick the top two.

- Try them for a few weeks. When you have a decision to make, an action to take, run it past your values – does it fit?

- If yes, keep it; if not, switch it out.

- Repeat until you've found your fit.

Reminder: your values will not be engraved on your tombstone (unless you want them to be). You can change your mind.

Another reason not to listen to customers is when the opportunity is too small. When the numbers just don't add up. But to figure that out, you need to do the maths first...

Reason 2: When the rewards are teeny-weeny

Sometimes your customers want something, but the rewards are so small you need a magnifying glass to see them. When an opportunity arises, doing your maths is paramount. Back of an envelope calculation works just fine. What you'll need to find out:

- How much is this going to cost me to create? (Think time and/or materials depending on whether you're a service or product business.)
- What additional costs have I forgotten? (Hiring space, postage, renting, childcare, digital subscriptions, etc.)
- At what price will I need to sell my offer to make a profit? (Get a range in your head.)
- How many will I need to sell? (Map out different scenarios with different price/volume.)
- How willing will my target audience be to pay the price I have in mind? (See testing price advice back in Chapter 11.)
- How much investment (time and money) is needed to market my product to the right people? That said, some folks can afford to make a loss in the early days. If they believe they can scale and eventually turn a profit. Maybe you have a loan, a financial cushion, generous parents or a partner who can cover the bills. Whatever your situation, be honest with yourself upfront. Before you get excited, always do the maths.

Reason 3: Someone else is doing it (much) better

Maybe someone, somewhere is already doing that thing your customers are asking for. And doing it damn well. Your customers are only ever a few clicks away from finding that out for themselves. Unless you have a rock-solid differentiator, don't go there. Always do your competitor research first. Remember Google is your friend (and not just page one of Google) and it's hard to dethrone a solid competitor. If you're going to go for it, you'll need a solid differentiator, something that helps you stand out. So, don't let someone else doing it put you off altogether. There are thousands of companies offering very similar things. Just be super-confident you've got a strong enough differentiator to pull it off.

Examples of differentiators:

- You. All that talk about you being unique, well it's true
- Targeting an underserved niche audience (e.g. women with ADHD, divorcees, bilingual families, etc.)
- Price point
- Language
- Environmental credentials

Be different. Otherwise, don't do it.

Reason 4: You just don't want to do it

Wow. There is power in saying no. Even if people are willing to throw money at us, we might not want to do it. You could give me ALL the money in the world, but I wouldn't go back to gutting chickens (student job, long story…). Many of us end up offering things we no longer enjoy doing even if we're getting paid for it. So, whether it's quitting quietly (or loudly) say no to things that no longer work for you. Don't hold back on batting off requests from customers for things you know (in your bones) you will not enjoy. Own the NO.

Reason 5: You don't have the bandwidth

You cannot do ALL the things. No seriously. There is always a catch. The frazzled, overworked small business owner is a thing, people! Forty-two per cent of small business owners report experiencing some form of burnout over the last six months.[2] Running small businesses can be exhausting. And that's without all the other things that are important or need to be done: your family, your relationships, your dog and all that life admin. You may think being your own boss meant nobody telling you how to spend your time. I must confess I often find myself reminiscing about the times my boss used to tell me what was important, what I needed to prioritize and what I needed to delegate. The truth is we're not that good at being in charge of our own time. So many requests and ideas. *You should do a podcast. You should start a newsletter. You should create a course. You should set up a shop on Etsy.* You should. You should. You should. Enough. If there is only you, or you have a tight team, think about whether you can feasibly fit in that extra thing customers want. What will you have to stop doing to be able to start doing the new thing? We are not machines.

To sum up

Customers can be our compass. Absolutely. But you need your own too. You want to be broadly heading (or should I say *hearting*) in a similar direction. If not, it sucks. And any joy you had will melt like a lolly on a hot day. Right. Back to listening to customers. In the final chapter of this book, *Three ways to make it happen and staying on the right side of the law,*

---

[2] E. Segal, *How burnout and inflation continue to impact small business owners*, Forbes (May 2022). Available from: www.forbes.com/sites/edwardsegal/2022/05/04/how-burnout-and-inflation-continue-to-impact-small-business-owners

I've giving you three options to help you weave market research into your business. I'll also make sure you stay on the right side of the law (and ethics) when it comes to research and give you some tips on when to consider hiring in the pros.

Chapter 12 recap:

- You don't always have to listen to your customers.

- Figure out your business values (stretch task #6) and make them your North Star.

- Do your maths (is this financially viable?).

- Keep an eye on the competition.

- Always ask yourself: Do I want to do this? Do I have the bandwidth?

13 Three ways to make it happen and staying on the right side of the law

I think on my feet. I once had to convince the CEO that throwing more people at the project I was running would NOT speed it up. Do you need more developers? I'll pay for that, he said. Do you need more testers? I'll pay for that. Sometimes more people speed things up. Not always.

I wracked my brain for an analogy. Imagine a small space, I told him. A bathroom you're renovating. The project manager says it'll take five weeks. Skill wise, you'll need a painter, a plumber, an electrician, a plasterer and someone to fit the fancy underfloor heating.

Paying everyone to come in at the same time will not cut that five-week timeline to a week. Do you see? There's an order: a start, a middle and an end. You cannot do the painting before you've done the plastering. You don't let the electrician in when the plumber is doing their thing.

The CEO? I won him over.

The analogy is powerful for businesses too. By all means, throw everything at your business. Do the courses, join the memberships and work on your mindset. But there's an order. Some foundations to get right. Learning how to understand your customers is THE foundational skill that makes the other choices, the other steps easier.

Extract from Jungle Juice, 14th January 2022

Chapter 13, our final chapter. We made it. The question at the heart of this last section is how do you go from reading this book to making market research happen in your businesses? It needs to be pragmatic and doable. Otherwise, I know it won't happen (I'm a small business too!). In this last chapter, I'm giving you three ways to do just that. These options are not prescriptive, and you don't need to follow them by the letter. Pick 'n' mix and amend and tweak as you see fit. But it's always better to start with something. It's how change (however small) happens.

All three options can be downloaded from www. productjungle.co.uk/book/resources.

Option 1: The stone

If you're starting small and solid.

Market research activity	Frequency	Detail
Survey (Chapter 7)	Annual	Commit to sending at least one survey a year. It could be to a subset of your community

		(newsletter subscribers, workshop attendees, someone who has bought one of your products). Remember to have a clear survey purpose and pay attention to your questions.
Desk research (Chapter 8)	Bi-annual (twice a year)	Schedule two desk research sessions into your calendar. Carve out the time in advance (it makes it more likely to happen!). Sessions can be between 30–60 minutes. Save relevant reports and insights into your Market Research folder (go create one already!).
Social-listening tools (Chapter 9)	Quarterly	Once every three months, fire up some of the tools and sites I recommended and get customer eavesdropping.
Customer interviews (Chapters 4, 5 & 6)	Annual	Commit to conducting at least one annual exploratory customer interview sprint*. Open your diary and schedule it in three to six months in advance. Think about it as separate blocks of time: time to decide on a high-level goal; time to craft questions; time to find folks to speak to; time to conduct the interviews; and time to make sense of it all.
Testing (Chapter 11)	As required	Check out the different tests you could run in Chapter 11. Remember to test small.
Feedback (Chapter 10)	Annual, then ongoing	Annual audit of your current feedback channels. One-off session of 1–2 hours.

		Then fill in any identified gaps. E.g. add feedback link to email signature, website, create stock feedback questions you can send following a purchase, or project completion.
Question Bank (Chapter 3)	Ongoing	Create an online or offline folder or document called Question Bank. Every time you start wondering something about your audience, bank the question. Your deposits can fuel your surveys and interviews.
Incentive budget	Optional	Set aside a small amount (£2–£5) each month to build an incentive pot. Incentives can be used to encourage customers and thank them for their input and time.

*A sprint is a predefined length of time when you commit to getting something done. Taken from agile software methodology.

Option 2: The peach

Ready to juice up your tempo? Give the peach option a try.

Activity	Frequency	Detail
Survey (Chapter 7)	Bi-annual (twice a year)	Commit to sending two surveys a year. It could be to a subset of your community (newsletter subscribers, workshop attendees, someone who has bought one of your products before). Remember to have a clear survey purpose. One could be more high level and the other more targeted and slightly shorter. Pay attention to your questions.

Desk research (Chapter 8)	Quarterly	Schedule four desk research sessions into your calendar. Carve out the time in advance (it makes it more likely to happen). Sessions can be between 30–60 minutes. Save reports and any insights into your Market Research folder. You will get faster as you start to know where to look. Don't forget to save your sources.
Social-listening tools (Chapter 9)	Bi-monthly (every two months)	Once every two months, fire up some of the recommended tools and sites. Let's get eavesdropping!
Customer interviews (Chapters 4, 5 & 6)	Bi-annual (twice a year)	Commit to conducting at least two customer interview sprints per year. Open your diary and schedule both of them in for three and six months' time. Think about it in blocks of time: time to decide on a goal; time to craft questions; time to find folks to speak to; time to conduct the interviews; and time to make sense of it all. One sprint could be exploratory, the other contextual.
Testing (Chapter 11)	As required	Check out the different tests you could use in Chapter 11. Remember to test small.
Feedback (Chapter 10)	Bi-annual (twice a year), then ongoing	Bi-annual audit of your feedback channels. Two, one-off sessions of 2–3 hours. Then fill in the gaps. E.g. add feedback to email signature, website, create stock feedback questions you can send following a purchase or project completion. Create a feedback

		list where you make note of anything action worthy. Follow up with customers to thank them (not just for the good feedback!).
Question Bank (Chapter 3)	Ongoing	Create an online or offline folder or document called Question Bank. Every time you start wondering something about your audience, bank the question. You can create your Question Bank without having any questions. Actively refer to your Question Bank ahead of drafting any survey or interview questions.
Incentive budget	Optional	Set aside a small amount (£2–£5) each month to build an incentive pot. Incentives can be used to encourage and thank customers for their input and time. Access as and when needed.

Option 3: The penguin

Already on a roll? Have a team to support you? Level up with the penguin.

Activity	Frequency	Detail
Survey (Chapter 7)	Bi-annual (twice a year) + one automated survey	Commit to sending two surveys a year. It could be to a subset of your community (newsletter subscribers, workshop attendees, someone who has bought one of your products before).

		One could be high level, the other more targeted and shorter. Remember to have a clear survey purpose and to pay attention to your questions. Add a third, automated survey to a key customer touchpoint to create a continuous feedback channel (after purchase, after project completion, etc.).
Desk research (Chapter 8)	Bi-monthly (every two months)	Schedule six desk research sessions into your calendar. Carve out the time in advance (it makes it more likely to happen). Sessions can be 30–60 minutes. Save reports and any insights into your Market Research folder. Make your life easier by signing up to alerts, notifications and emails from relevant bodies.
Social-listening tools (Chapter 9)	Monthly	As little as 60 minutes a month using the recommended tools and sites can generate content ideas and identify new trends.
Customer interviews (Chapters 4, 5 & 6)	Continuous	Schedule in short (think 15–30 minutes) conversations with customers on a regular basis. Start with a commitment to one call a month with the aim of building up that frequency. Think creatively. This could be a few pertinent questions at the end of an existing client 1:1 or a short chat with a prospective customer at the local market. Commit to two, meatier customer discovery sprints during the year (either exploratory or

		contextual). Plan for this higher cadence in advance. Open your diary and schedule the associated tasks. Think about the time it will take to secure interviews and draft questions and note opportunities you already have with customers.
Testing (Chapter 11)	As required	Check out the different tests you could use in Chapter 11. Remember test small.
Feedback (Chapter 10)	Quarterly, then ongoing	Quarterly audit of feedback channels. Maintain a feedback list and ensure to inform customers of changes you've made as a result (e.g. You said, we did…). Keep checking the basics such as adding feedback options to email signature, website. Create stock request-feedback questions you can send customers after a project or a purchase and review and tweak regularly.
Question Bank (Chapter 3)	Ongoing	Create an online or offline folder or document called Question Bank. Every time you start wondering something about your audience, bank the question.
Incentive budget	Monthly	With this level of activities, you'll need to commit to setting aside a small amount (£5–£10) each month to build an incentive pot. Incentives can be used to encourage and thank customers for their input and time.

Pick the right *option* for you and start to understand your customers better.

Staying on the right side of the law

Small is not above the law when it comes to customer data and privacy. There are rules to follow when engaging with customers and handling their information. Good enough won't quite cut it. But don't be scared off. Most of the guidance is common sense. The MRS is the industry reference when it comes to research standards. Its code of conduct governs research activities.[1] I've selected the most important points for businesses doing their own research below. This is by no means an exhaustive list and when in doubt, do seek out further guidance. And always remember to check the data and privacy laws in your country of residence:

- Wherever possible, those who take part must be told the purpose of the research.
- The right to privacy must be respected. People who take part must not be identified without their agreement and they must not be harmed or embarrassed as a result of taking part.
- You must anonymize the information you collect as much as possible, unless given consent.
- You must store any customer information in a secure location and not keep it for longer than necessary.
- You must obtain consent to an interview being recorded. You'll also need consent for observations.
- Any assurances you make about the interview, including how long it will take, must be factually correct.

---

[1] Market Research Society (MRS), *Code of conduct*, mrs.org.uk (May 2023). Available from: www.mrs.org.uk/standards/code-of-conduct

- When interviewing children (under 16), you must get prior permission from a responsible adult, such as a parent, guardian, teacher, grandparent or caregiver.
- If you promise an incentive to participants, this promise must be honoured. Incentives should not constitute or be perceived to constitute a bribe.

You can find links to the latest MRS code of conduct in the useful links section at the end of the book.

When to hire the pros

There will be situations when calling in expertise is the right thing to do. Investing in professional market research support can accelerate discovery and get you reliable answers faster. It can help navigate hard-to-reach audiences, negotiate different cultures and markets, and increase your chances of survey success with skilfully crafted questions.

Below are a few situations where you could consider calling in some pro help.

- **Investment**. If you are looking to raise *serious* money from investors (or the bank), you'll need to show you've done some customer homework. Having support from a research professional ensures you get the right insights, in the right format, to reassure investors you *know* what makes your customers tick.
- **Marketing and branding**. Copywriting for your website, ads or offers are difficult to get right alone. If your copy isn't generating the results you expected, it might be time to seek professional help. Good copywriters will always start with your customer.
- **New launch**. The more money you plan to invest in launching something, the greater the risk of losing it if

you get things wrong. Do yourself a favour and get the help you need if you are thinking *big*, big.

- **New market**. Imagine you want to enter the Chinese market. Unless you're a Chinese market expert, you'll need some help. Same for any other new market you wish to enter. It will avoid costly mistakes down the line.
- **Large surveys**. If you need a large sample size, survey specialists can help get your questions in front of the right audience. They can also make sure you get the most out of your questions.
- **Discussion guide**. Sometimes we just need a little support crafting quality questions. Some independent market research specialists can support with making sure you get the most out of your customer interviews (brilliant questions = better insights).

Investing in professional help doesn't mean washing your hands of the whole process. Stay as close as you can and listen in to conversations where possible, even if someone else is interviewing. Keep tabs on data coming in. Remember that customer insights are always more powerful first-hand. Finally, choosing the right partner needn't be daunting. After reading this book, you have a solid enough idea of what good research looks like. Here are a few questions I recommend you ask if, and when, you select a market research partner for your business:

- Have you worked with small businesses in the past?
- What experience do you have working with my type of target customer/industry?
- What types of insights did you deliver and in what format?
- How do you go about recruiting participants/ accessing audiences?
- How will I know that you are targeting the right people?

- What will the project deliverables look like?
- What feedback do you give on my research goal?

MRS has a handy directory of accredited market research service providers on their website.[2] The list includes boutique agencies, independent freelancers and some of the biggest names in research. MRS also have handy guidance on selecting a partner. An excellent place to start.

To sum up

This final chapter answered the crucial question *What now?* I gave you three options. Each option contains all the research methods covered in this book with varying degrees of intensity. Pick the one best suited to your situation. More importantly, pick one you can maintain and don't bite off more than you can chew. Once you've made your pick, why not print it out and pin it to your wall? A visible plan of action is always more likely to happen. This chapter also highlighted the rules and guidelines to follow when interacting with customers for research purposes. A bit of rigour goes a long way. Always keep your customers informed of your research intentions and keep their data safe.

Chapter 13 recap:

- Pick a market research option that works for you.

- Print it out and pin it up somewhere visible.

- Consult the MRS code of conduct to keep your research activities the right side of the law.

---

[2] Market Research Society (MRS), *Research buyers guide*, mrs.org.uk. Available from: www.mrs.org.uk/researchbuyersguide

- Consider hiring professional researchers for higher risk projects, large surveys and market research in brand-new markets.

- Find MRS accredited research professionals suitable for your budget on the MRS website.

Conclusion

I kissed 1,000 Frenchmen.

The calculations are approximate. But between 1989 and 1999, I kissed 1,000 Frenchmen. Now… hold your horses. In France, the four-kiss greeting – la bise for the initiated – has always been *de rigueur* in Northwest France.

My recent trip served up a whole different experience. COVID-19 changed habits forged over centuries. Leaning in to greet the elders, I was presented with an elbow. Stooping low to greet the kids, a fist (pump).

Change.

Things change. However tight we hold onto behaviours… change is lurking in the side-lines like COVID-19 on a (public) handrail. But impermanence is where innovation so often lies.

What's changed for your audience? What givens are forgone? What certainties are slowly sinking? Change is the only constant. Sometimes sudden. Sometimes slow. Always an opportunity.

Extract from Jungle Juice, 18th April 2022

The thing is, in business, as in life, there are no guarantees. Everything is always shifting. People. Culture. The economy. Ourselves. It's called impermanence. Market research as a practice can be an anchor to tether you back to a repeatable practice. A practice that gets you one step closer to your customers, to the people you serve. Because without them, there is no business. If you're not probing, poking, asking and checking (more of the time), you're guessing.

Market research doesn't have to be perfect. Understanding customers never is. Customers are humans. They are messy, flawed, unpredictable and irrational. But with the right mindset, intention, tools and skills you *can* make sense of them. Enough sense to make better decisions. To move forward with more clarity. To fail faster and create stuff that people want and buy. You won't ever have all the answers, but each time you lean in, you'll *get* a few more. Chief Insight Officer at Categoracle, Tori Rosevink, summed it up perfectly: 'There's not one *right* way to do market research. The only wrong way is not to do it at all.'

This book gave you more than a peach to chew on. So, take what you need now, and come back when you need more. Starting small is still starting. Tweak the survey you plan to send this month. Set time aside (like for real) to get some desk research done. Take the online tools I mentioned for a spin. Have a big idea? Set up customer interviews and craft good questions. Feeling lost? Ditto. As for testing, think nimble and lightweight. Always asking yourself, *What is the smallest and most useful thing I can put out into the world that'll teach me something?*

Intentionally talking to customers feels like the final frontier for smaller businesses. Most of you have sent a survey, read a trend report, but few of you are interviewing customers as a business practice. Let that be this book's biggest takeaway. Talk to your people. Big businesses are increasingly splashing the cash doing just *that* and more. They have books written FOR them. Specialist consultants, researchers and agencies creating strategies FOR them. They are diligently building teams of experts. Don't be intimidated. On the contrary, let this empower you. The tools and methods used in big business will work in your business too.

Never forget small has advantages. Small means closer to your customer, more trustworthy and authentic. Small means nimble and has already crossed the finish line… while *big* is so often still jumping through the first (corporate) hoop. Our world needs small.

Running a small business, being your own boss, freelancing and making a living from it is hard work. Far from being another item on the never-ending to-do list, let market research relieve some of the burden. Think of this book as your map in the maze. Even with the map in your hand, you're still bound to take a few wrong turns, but you'll make it out faster than without.

To finish, let's come back to Jane Frost CBE, CEO of MRS. 'Market research is not rocket science. It's respect.' You, your business and your customers deserve no less. So, stay curious. Bank those questions. Be brave. Keep leaning into your customers. In these turbulent times, the answers so often lie with them. But we need to ask.

My hope is you finish this book a little wiser, a little braver and a little more curious. Do tell me how you get on. Long after you put this book down, I'll still be here. Rooting for you and for your customers and for all your brilliant businesses.

As for our question *Do penguins eat peaches?* Let's go find out…

Until next time…

Do penguins eat peaches?

Do penguins eat peaches? What a curious question. When we move past the obvious, what answers did we get? From AI to Managing Directors (MDs) with a few kids in-between… some of my favourite answers for you are here.

I guess penguins don't normally eat peaches because they can't normally get them. So, if you asked them, the answer would be no. But the answer might be yes if you could introduce them to the idea, since after all I would hate to assume a penguin's answer!

Michael Dell, MD of Maritime Intelligence

No, they've never seen one, heard of them or eaten one. And, because they live in the Arctic and peaches live in the normal human realm, they've never heard of it or seen it so they can't eat it can they?

Grace, 8

No, penguins do not eat peaches. Penguins are birds that feed primarily on fish, squid and krill. Their digestive systems and diets are adapted to consume seafood, so they do not typically eat fruit like peaches. In theory, a penguin could eat a peach, but it would not provide any nutritional value for them as their digestive systems are not designed to process fruit. It could also potentially cause digestive issues for the penguin. It is best for penguins to stick to their natural diet of seafood.

ChatGPT (Artificial Intelligence)

It's too cold for peach trees to live there. They need heat to live so that's why they can't eat peaches. There's another answer too; because if they were pecking into it, they'd probably accidently eat the stone, which would get stuck in their throat and kill them.

Errol, 8

My gut reaction is to say no. However, penguins could have been introduced to peaches when in captivity. Possibly in a zoo or within a conservation context? So technically, yes, a penguin could well have eaten a peach.

Jessica Weiss, analyst and researcher

They don't eat peaches because they're too big and round and hard [the peaches] and they [penguins] wouldn't be able to peck it.

Seren, 6

Product Jungle offers a range of Market Research and Product Management services including:

PRODUCT JUNGLE

- Consulting
- Mentoring
- Training
- Workshops
- Keynote and Headline Speaking

For more information go to www.productjungle.co.uk or email letstalk@productjungle.co.uk

Keep customers front of mind and join hundreds of businesses on the Jungle Juice mailing list.

Weekly tips, advice and stories helping you understand customers better.

Scan the QR code to sign up.

If you enjoyed this book, please do nip over to Amazon or your favourite independent book retailer and leave a review. It helps other like-minded readers find their way to *Do Penguins Eat Peaches?* I really appreciate it.

The End

Question Bank

Here are a list of questions and question stems to use when talking to customers. You can find a digital version on my website: www.productjungle.co.uk/book/resources. Looking for further inspiration? Caroline Wilson runs the research and insights business Vireo Research and drops weekly question magic in her newsletter. To sign up visit: https://vireoresearch. com/vireo-asks

Make sure you create your own Question Bank with real questions relevant to your business and your natural way of talking. Every time you ask yourself, *I wonder whether my customer...* bank it.

- Tell me about...
- Talk me through the last time you...
- Run me through a typical...
- How would you normally go about...?
- Walk me through how you...?
- How often are you able to successfully...?
- How do you feel when...?
- What steps would you take to...?
- What does success look like for you when...?
- Talk me through the last time something went badly wrong when...
- How long does it normally take you to...?
- How much time would you ideally like to spend on it?

- How are you solving that problem/challenge today?
- How often would you say that happens?
- How many times a day/week/month/year does that occur?
- Does it take you an hour a day or more like five minutes? (this question is for narrowing down time scales when someone answers 'it depends')
- How do you feel about how long it currently takes you?
- What would you be doing instead if this wasn't taking you this long?
- How much do you currently spend trying to solve this challenge?
- How do you feel about that cost?
- Thinking about all the frustrations when it comes to [insert as appropriate] what is the worst one?
- If you could do [insert as appropriate] in half the time, what would that change for you?
- What shortcuts and workarounds do you currently use to do [insert as appropriate]?
- How effective are they?
- Why is that do you think?
- Could you tell me a bit more about that?
- That's interesting, why do you think that is?
- Can you rank the challenges you mentioned from one to five?
- Can you rank these benefits you mentioned from one to five?
- Of all the challenges you mentioned, when trying to do [insert as appropriate], which one would be the most useful to solve?
- If you had a magic wand, which of the current challenges you mentioned would you make disappear?
- How frequently do you have to do it?
- What is the most frustrating part of doing...?

- How does that compare to the other frustrations you've mentioned when doing...?
- What is the most rewarding part of doing...?
- What does good look like when you...?

Themes to explore with customers

Here is a list of suggested themes to explore with customers.

- Sustainability
- Accessibility
- Neurodiversity
- Diversity and inclusion
- Hybrid working
- Learning styles and habits
- Work life balance
- Decision making
- Wellbeing

Useful links

Enterprise Nation: www.enterprisenation.com

Federation of Small Businesses (FSB): www.fsb.org.uk

Gabor-Granger pricing model: www.surveyking.com/help/gabor-granger

Google Scholar: https://scholar.google.com

Grain: www.grain.com

Hub Spot: www.hubspot.com

Ipsos: www.ipsos.com/en-uk

Mintel: www.mintel.com

MRS code of conduct: www.mrs.org.uk/standards/code-of-conduct

Quora: www.quora.com

Reddit: www.reddit.com

Statistica: www.statista.com

Survey Monkey sample size calculator: www.surveymonkey.com/mp/sample-size-calculator

The UK Office for National Statistics (ONS): www.ons.gov.uk

Think with Google: www.thinkwithgoogle.com

Trade bodies and associations – Trade Association Forum: www.taforum.org

Van Westendorp: www.surveyking.com/help/van-westendorp-analysis

Contributor bios

Find out more about the smart minds I interviewed for this book.

Adam Forbes is an advisor to corporates, start-ups and individuals, as well as founder of Familiarize, a marketing consultancy for small and medium sized businesses, and is a programme director and mentor for the global accelerator, Startupbootcamp. He has spent more than 25 years working in and with large corporate organizations in marketing, business development and innovation, always with an eye on creating value for the customer.

Adam Forbes

Sara is the CEO of Outwitly Inc. and a design strategist. She is an expert in ethnographic research methods, UX and service design. She is passionate about human-centred approaches to innovation. Prior to founding Outwitly, Sara worked in Silicon Valley for Fortune 500 clients such as Apple, AT&T and Microsoft. She is also the former UX Director for one of the top 10 media companies in the US where she led the consumer products design and research teams.

Sara Fortier

Jane is CEO of the MRS. She moved into the research, data and insights sector after a career running the gamut from CMO to brand and strategy leadership. As Customer Director of HMRC she was awarded a CBE for the development of innovative corporate strategies based on deep customer insight. She also holds numerous creative and marketing awards from her time at Unilever, Shell and the BBC.

Jane Frost CBE

Diana is a serial entrepreneur who entered the United States as a refugee from Ukraine at the age of eight. By her early thirties, she'd launched and sold millions of dollars' worth of products and services. Today, she is an innovation consultant, keynote speaker and *New York Times* bestselling author whose books have been taught in over one hundred universities. She can juggle, do a handstand, though not at the same time... yet.

Diana Kander

Tamara is the founder of the pricing consultancy Nine Nine Lab. She has over seven years of experience building pricing strategies across industries ranging from e-commerce to AI and SaaS. With a Masters in Finance and an Undergraduate in Psychology, she understands the right mix of numbers and psychology that'll get you to a successful strategy. Her clients include Groupon, Wiggle, Lovecrafts, Elzin, Utilita and Finalis.

Tamara Milacic

Trina is a UX researcher and designer who started her career as a User Interface (UI) developer. She loves solving complex design challenges and spends most of her time learning how to design more inclusive experiences. When she is not writing, she enjoys watching social and cultural documentaries, live music and travelling.

Trina Moore Parvell

Lennart is a pioneer in games, gamification and user experience. As Professor of Human–Computer Interaction (HCI) in Games at University of Waterloo, he explores how user experience of video and exercise games can drive engagement and change behaviours. Over the past 15 years, he has published more than 200 academic papers and a bestselling book on Games User Research. A sought-after keynote speaker, Lennart has advised organizations worldwide on effective gamification strategies. He was recognized among the top 10 HCI scholars of the last decade and the top 2% of scientists worldwide. His groundbreaking work continues to shape how we understand and apply games research.

Dr Lennart Nacke

Nana Parry is a serial entrepreneur and the founder of Tectonic, a research firm that helps companies understand customers. He works with start-ups and FTSE250 companies with a client base spanning 12 different countries. Nana also runs a Venture Studio, helping large corporations create businesses from scratch. He lectures business students at Imperial College London, UCL, London Business School and Capital Enterprise. Prior to his founder journey, Nana worked for tech companies like Fujitsu and Rackspace, delivering multi-million-dollar projects and running large teams.

Nana Parry

Dana has consulted for NASA, McKinsey, Google, Virgin, Veeva and start-ups including MURAL, Andela, Butter, Prelo and UnderPinned. With a distinguished career in both customer research and award-winning copywriting, Dana is the founder and CEO of Publicover & Co, a growth marketing agency specializing in rapid and sustainable start-up growth. She is the author of *Empathy at Scale, How to Talk to Customers* and *DIY Marketing for Startups* and the ghost-writer of more than a dozen non-fiction titles. She is a US expat and lives in Hamburg, Germany.

Dana Publicover

Tori has spent her career understanding what people put in their baskets and why. Her early career was spent at Nielsen, focused on the 'what'; analysing sales performance, shopper behaviour and predicting innovation success for globally recognized brands. The 'why' came in 2018 when Tori went freelance and moved into emotion analytics; leveraging hybrid text analytics and online reviews to discover how people feel about products, and why, so innovators can meet real customer needs.

Tori Rosevink

Jonny is a product leader with a background in product management, experience strategy and digital innovation. He's got lots of consulting experience (ThoughtWorks, AWS), and has worked in staff teams too (Amazon). He is the author of *Understanding Design Thinking, Lean, and Agile* (O'Reilly, 2017). Jonny lives in Melbourne, consults globally and makes fine furniture in his spare time.

Jonny Schneider

Caroline has over 20 years' experience taking complex business challenges from the world's largest brands and finding solutions. She started her career in financial services data and then the retail world, before moving into senior research agency roles. In 2009, she opened Vireo Research, and in 2019 she launched a product and online store for neurodiverse kids and their parents. She's also a board member and former college instructor. She loves to chat about research and data as the solution to many of our big decisions, but also other important stuff like the best snacks, neurodivergent parenting and growing your own food.

Caroline Wilson

To find out more about their current work (and see their smiling faces) head to www.productjungle.co.uk/book/contributors

Acknowledgements

I t takes a village to write a book. Here's mine.

First, a huge thanks to Alison Jones, her team, and partners at Practical Inspiration Publishing (PIP) for believing in my idea. For their guidance and support. And for giving me the opportunity to put a book into the world, a hard-fought dream come true. Thank you.

A special thanks to my girlfriends. You believed in me, encouraged me and listened to me bang on about writing a book, long before a deal came along. You cheered me on from the side-lines when you already had so much going on in your own lives. Caroline B, Isabel S, Karin H, Mirja E, Jennie F and Ahlisha D, thank you. Each one of you has supported me in your own unique way over the last few years. Forever grateful.

To my Clockwise crew: Anneliese L, Sam B, Nicky D, Karlene H, Julie V, Jess W and Phil B and all you others I pestered while writing this book. Co-working was the best decision I took in lockdown. Thanks for your honest feedback, your listening ears and all the wonderful conversations. And a big thanks to the team at Clockwise, North London, for creating a space where I want to write.

To my beta readers: Jo M, Isabel S, Karin H, Laetitia T, Adam F, Jessica CC, Anne F, Sue M, Liz R and Dad. Your feedback made it a better book.

To my Instagram pals who have been rooting for me ever since I mentioned putting a book out into the world. I learnt so much about small businesses from you. You've all had an impact on how this book turned out. Thank you.

To my Jungle Juice community. Sending you my newsletter week-in-week-out, getting your heart-felt feedback on my words made me fall in love with writing again. Thank you.

To my business coach Ruth for bringing Alison and her business book challenge to my attention all those years ago. For always telling me that what I wanted was possible and nudging me in the right direction.

To my virtual (and very real) assistant Chantal who lightened my load so I could focus on writing.

And to the many others who have been part of my career journey to now. Clients, former colleagues and managers.

To all the contributors quoted and referenced in this book: Jane Frost CBE, Adam Forbes, Sara Fortier, Diana Kander, Tamara Milacic, Trina Moore Pervall, Dr Lennart Nacke, Nana Parry, Dana Publicover, Tori Rosevink, Jonny Schneider and Caroline Wilson. Thanks for your generous wisdom, time and insights. My book is stronger thanks to you all.

A special thanks to Anne-Laure Le Cunff and folks at the MRS for giving me permission to share their work. To Emma George, Lara Sheldrake and Belinda Knott for letting me use their businesses as examples in this book and to all the others that inspired my fictional examples.

To all my endorsers. Thanks for penning those wonderful lines of support and for not blocking my email address (I can be persistent!).

Thanks and appreciation to all the authors and experts I have referenced in this book (standing on the shoulders of giants and all that...).

To you, dear reader, for picking up this book and taking a punt on a first-time author.

To Mum and Dad, always there for me and believing I'd write a book one day. Thanks for all the adventures, the soulful chats and making me brave and curious. A big thanks to my siblings and their families: Oliver, Suguna, Jayana, Shanti, Victoria, Erin and Thomas. Thanks for never begrudging me for not answering messages, forgetting birthdays and failing to post the Christmas presents on time. Writing a book is all consuming. And a special thanks to Eve for all your kind words of support.

To my French family and friends across the Channel: Geneviève, Bernard, Alexandra, Laurine, Esteban, Magali, Bérengère and Blandine. Thank you for the welcome, the conversations, the food and for bearing with me while I try to explain, in French, why I called my book *Do Penguins Eat Peaches?*

An extra special thanks to my two awesome children: Aidan and Grace. They never let *author* get to my head. Provided unfiltered and sometimes unsolicited feedback on peripheral topics such as time management, book cover design and the type of books I should be writing next. I am so proud of you. And I LOVE you.

And saving the most important thank you until last. To David. A brilliant man. Always by my side, quietly believing in me. I couldn't have done this without you. *Merci pour tout…*

Katie, London 2023

Index

A quick word from Practical Inspiration Publishing...

We hope you found this book both practical and inspiring – that's what we aim for with every book we publish.

We publish titles on topics ranging from leadership, entrepreneurship, HR and marketing to self-development and wellbeing.

Find details of all our books at: www.practicalinspiration.com

 Did you know...

We can offer discounts on bulk sales of all our titles – ideal if you want to use them for training purposes, corporate giveaways or simply because you feel these ideas deserve to be shared with your network.

We can even produce bespoke versions of our books, for example with your organization's logo and/or a tailored foreword.

To discuss further, contact us on info@practicalinspiration.com.

 Got an idea for a business book?

We may be able to help. Find out more about publishing in partnership with us at: bit.ly/PIpublishing.

Follow us on social media...

🐦 @PIPTalking

📷 @pip_talking

📘 @practicalinspiration

🎵 @piptalking

in Practical Inspiration Publishing

Printed in the USA
CPSIA information can be obtained
at www.ICGtesting.com
JSHW012127061023
49815JS00010B/32